winter food

For Elinor, with love

Jill Norman

winter food

seasonal recipes for the colder months

Photography by Jason Lowe

Kyle Cathie Limited

Author's note

Good cooking starts with good shopping. Buy the best quality you can afford, and let your menu be guided by what looks best. Farmers' markets are a great source of fresh, seasonal foods.

Stores of dried or canned foods are useful accompaniments to fresh ingredients, to add flavour or provide a shortcut. Beans and grains, spices and a few dried herbs, dried mushrooms, anchovies and olives, mustard, oils and vinegars, tinned tomatoes, soy and chilli sauce, chocolate, nuts and dried fruits are among my essentials.

Chicken and fish stock are easy to make at home or they can be bought. I buy meat stock and for vegetable stock use Marigold granules – these give a far better flavour than chopped and simmered vegetable offcuts.

I prefer unsalted butter for cooking, and use good-quality olive oil that imparts a flavour, or flavourless sunflower oil. Amounts of herbs and spices are specified, but can be adjusted to suit your taste. My dishes are not heavily salted, and some have no salt at all because other flavourings are adequate.

The recipes give the basic method for preparing a dish, and most are capable of variation. Food evolves all the time, a dish changes from one region to another, from one cook to another. As long as the idea of a dish is respected, we should feel free to interpret the recipe according to our own palate and imagination.

I have only used metric measures in the recipes, because these are now the weights and measures used in daily shopping. You can find imperial equivalents on page 188.

First published in Great Britain in 2005 by Kyle Cathie Limited, 122 Arlington Road, London NW1 7HP
general.enquiries@kyle-cathie.com
www.kylecathie.com

ISBN 1 85626 562 5

The quotation from Philip Larkin's 'Winter Nocturne' is taken from his *Collected Poems* and reprinted by permission of Faber & Faber Ltd.

Project editor Caroline Taggart   Art direction and design by Vanessa Courtier
Home economy by Sunil Vijayakar   Styling by Vanessa Courtier and Jason Lowe
Copy editor Vanessa Kendell   Production by Sha Huxtable, Geoff Barlow and Alice Holloway

Jill Norman is hereby identified as the author of this work in accordance with Section 77 of the Copyright, Designs and Patents Act 1988.

A Cataloguing in Publication record for this title is available from the British Library.

Printed and bound in Singapore through Tien-Wah Press

Contents

Introduction

Mantled in grey, the dusk steals slowly in,
Crossing the dead, dull fields with footsteps cold.
The rain drips drearily; night's fingers spin
A web of drifting mist o'er wood and wold

Philip Larkin, *Winter Nocturne.*

It is, beyond doubt, an English winter that Larkin is describing: grey, dreary and dank. It is the kind of winter that I loathe; miserable and depressing, it wipes the smiles from people's faces, makes them huddle in their clothes.

Dry cold, bright skies and snow are a different matter. I remember walking in Moscow in mid-winter, snow piled in towering banks along the pavements, the temperature well below zero, and seeing, with amazement, people eating ice cream. The kiosks were doing brisk business; I joined a queue; the ice cream was excellent (unlike most Russian food at that time) and I was converted to the pleasure of ice cream in winter. I remembered, too, reading of snow helva made on the Anatolian plateau in Turkey and of a Russian recipe using snow in pancakes.

Back home, I pondered our own attitudes to winter food. In the general gloom we tend to neglect the delicacies winter has to offer: prime shellfish and seafood; extravagant truffles; geese, the only domestic bird remaining seasonal; succulent Vacherin du Mont d'Or, made from rich winter milk. None of these is ever welcomed with the enthusiasm aroused by the first asparagus or local strawberries.

Until less than a century ago, once the harvest was in, cooks used to spend long hours preserving its bounty for winter. Meat and fish were salted, smoked, pickled or dried; vegetables salted or pickled; fruit made into jams and preserves. The larder shelves were filled with cheeses, crocks and jars, dried beans and peas; a sack of potatoes, a barrel of sauerkraut stood on the floor; a flitch of bacon, a ham or cured sausages hung from the ceiling. The houses of the rich also had a game larder, away from the house so that unpleasant smells were contained.

Refrigeration removed much of the need to preserve foods, and modern houses seldom have larders, but our shelves still hold grains and dried or tinned beans, dried herbs and fruit, pickles and preserves. Nor have we lost our taste for smoked salmon, a fine ham or spiced beef.

Winter vegetables are often despised as a collection of dull roots and cabbages, and dull they may be if not treated well, but the earthy aromas of roasting root vegetables and the rich scent of caramelised onions add warmth to the season and will draw you into the kitchen. The creamy flavours of a Russian cabbage pie or the crunchy texture of spiced red cabbage belie the 'boiled-to-death' image often associated with the brassicas. While gardens, orchards and fields lie dormant, quinces and pomegranates, walnuts and chestnuts, pumpkins and other squashes provide lively colours and flavours for the cook well into winter. Forests and moors may be in the grip of cold, but there the hunt provides us with partridge, wild duck, venison and hare.

Winter food should be comforting and sustaining to counteract dark and damp. Nothing lifts the spirit more, after trudging through icy wind or chilling rain, than a savoury soup or stew. These are the essence of winter food and, for that matter, also of peasant food: aromatic, robust and satisfying one-pot meals, best made in large quantities for a convivial meal with family or friends. Whatever the name – hotpot, goulash, daube, brasato, ragoût – these quickly prepared and slowly cooked dishes are the foods we most relish in winter.

Spices, too, come into their own in winter cooking. Originally, their volatile oils helped to prolong the life of many foods, and they were essential in celebratory meals. The shepherds in Shakespeare's *The Winter's Tale* needed spices for their sheep-shearing feast; first of all 'saffron to colour the warden (pear) pies'. Saffron brought brightness to the table when the sun had disappeared. Today we value spices for their scent, flavour and visual appeal, to bring life to slow-cooked dishes, coat meat and fish, provide colour for a soup, enhance a dessert, flavour mulled wine and hot toddies.

The recipes in this book use seasonal ingredients and offer a variety of dishes from different cultures. I have travelled widely to other wintry places and always returned with new ideas. From northern China, the high Andes, the plateaux of Spain and Turkey, the mountain villages of northern Italy as well as from Russia, Scandinavia and central Europe, there are rich and enticing dishes to counter winter's chill.

soups

Brussels sprout soup

In this pretty, pale green soup the sprouts are cooked following Escoffier's advice: to 'stew them in butter', then 'combine them with as much fresh cream as possible'. It gives them a subtle flavour.

serves 6

500g small Brussels sprouts

30g butter

1 tablespoon plain flour

3 large cloves garlic, chopped

1.25 litres hot chicken or
   vegetable stock

1 egg yolk

120ml double cream or
   crème fraîche

salt and freshly ground black pepper

pinch of nutmeg

croûtons, to serve

Blanch the sprouts in boiling water for 3 minutes and drain. Heat the butter in a large pan, add the sprouts and shake and toss them in the butter. Sprinkle over the flour and garlic, mix well and pour over the hot stock, stirring continually. Simmer until the sprouts are soft, about 20 minutes. Blend the soup until smooth.

Beat the egg yolk with the cream, pour a ladleful of soup into the mixture, then stir this mixture into the soup over a very low heat. Remove the pan from the heat and continue to stir for 1 minute. Season with salt, pepper and nutmeg and serve at once with croûtons.

Carrot and celery soup

A quickly made soup with a light, delicate flavour.

serves 4

400g carrots

200g celery

2–3 tablespoons olive oil

salt and freshly ground black pepper

1 litre vegetable or chicken stock

2 tablespoons chopped fresh dill or
   1 tablespoon dried

croûtons, to serve

Grate the carrots and celery, removing any tough strings from the celery as you do so. Heat the oil in a large pan and cook the vegetables gently for 15–20 minutes with the lid on. Stir them occasionally. Season with salt and pepper. Pour in the stock, bring to the boil, add most of the dill if fresh, all if dried, and simmer for 20 minutes. Blend three quarters of the soup and sieve. Combine this with the unblended soup and taste for seasoning. Garnish with the remaining fresh dill, if using, and serve with croûtons.

Lentil and mussel soup

This soup, which originated in the Belgian port of Ostend, is satisfying enough to serve as a main course. The earthiness of the lentils provides a good background for the delicate flavour of the mussels.

serves 6–8 as a first course,
4 as a main

300g brown or green lentils,
    rinsed well
1 small onion, sliced
1 stick celery, sliced
1 bay leaf
1.5 litres vegetable stock or water
freshly ground black pepper
½ teaspoon ground cumin
1 tablespoon lemon juice
1kg mussels
snipped chives, to garnish

Put the lentils into a large pan with the onion, celery, bay leaf and stock or water. Season with pepper and cumin, bring slowly to the boil, then cover and simmer until the lentils are soft, about 40 minutes. Remove from the heat and purée until smooth. Add the lemon juice.

While the lentils are cooking, scrub the mussels and remove the beards, discarding any that are broken or gaping open. Put the mussels in a large pan with 80ml of water, cover and steam, shaking the pan from time to time, until the shells open (discard any that don't). Drain into a colander set over a large bowl. Discard the shells and put the mussels into a bowl. Strain the mussel liquor through a very fine sieve or one lined with damp muslin.

Stir the mussels and liquor into the soup. If the soup is too thick, add a little water. Taste and adjust the seasoning; the mussels should add enough saltiness. Heat through gently, sprinkle over the chives and serve.

Variation
Instead of mussels, finish the soup with pieces of firm white fish, such as sea bass, halibut, monkfish or bream. Cut about 350g of fillet into pieces of 4–5cm, fry them for 2 minutes on each side in a little olive oil and add to the soup after it has been ladled into bowls. A more extravagant soup can be made by adding a poached and shelled langoustine to each serving.

Dutch pea soup

This warming and filling soup uses three different kinds of each of the main ingredients – pulses, meat, vegetables and bread. It may sound complicated, but in fact it is only the cooking time that is long, not the preparation, and it is well worth the effort. Serve it as a main dish.

If possible, make pea soup the day before you want to eat it: the soup will be much better. It may have gone very thick, but gentle heating will restore its fluidity – if necessary add a little more water.

serves 6

750g split green peas

3 leeks, chopped

bunch of herb celery, or 6 celery
   stalks, chopped

1 small celeriac, diced

salt and freshly ground black pepper

6 spare ribs

12 pork sausages

handful of dried whole green peas,
   soaked overnight and drained

handful of dried white beans,
   soaked overnight and drained

6 thick slices streaky bacon,
   rinds removed

6 slices each of good white, brown
   and pumpernickel bread,
   to serve

butter and mustard, to serve

Wash the split peas and put them in a large pan with 4 litres of water. Bring to the boil, skim off any scum, reduce the heat and simmer for about 3 hours. Check from time to time to make sure nothing sticks to the bottom and add more water if necessary. When the peas are quite soft, the contents of the pan will have become almost purée-like. If you like a very smooth soup, sieve it now and return it to the pan.

Stir the leeks, celery and celeriac into the soup and season to taste. Add the spare ribs and sausages, the peas and beans, and simmer all on a low heat for another 3 hours. After 2 hours, add the bacon. Check regularly that nothing sticks to the pan and add more water if needed.

Provide everyone with a soup plate, and a side plate for the meat. Put the different breads – white for the sausages; brown for the spare ribs; pumpernickel for the bacon – on the table alongside the butter, mustard and a peppermill. Bring the soup to the table in a large bowl and let everyone help themselves.

Butternut and split pea soup

I like the texture of butternut squash in this soup, but any squash or pumpkin can be used. Speck is German cured and smoked belly pork. It is sold in delicatessens, usually in thick pieces suitable for cutting into cubes.

serves 6–8

1 tablespoon sunflower oil

150g speck or smoked bacon, cubed

1 large onion, chopped

1 teaspoon ground coriander

1/2 teaspoon allspice

salt and freshly ground black pepper

150g yellow split peas

3 litres stock or water

800g butternut squash

2–3 spring onions, finely sliced,
    to garnish

Heat the oil in a large, heavy pan and sauté the speck until it starts to colour. Add the onion and continue to sauté until the onion is pale gold. Stir in the coriander, allspice and a good grinding of pepper, then add the split peas and pour in the stock. Bring to the boil, skim the surface if necessary, and simmer, covered, until the peas are soft, about 30 minutes.

Meanwhile, peel the butternut, discard the seeds and fibres and cut the flesh into small pieces. Add the squash to the liquid, bring it back to a simmer and cook until the squash is soft, about 15–20 minutes. Blend the soup and taste. If necessary, season with a little salt, but usually the speck provides all the salt needed. If the soup is too thick dilute it with a little water. Garnish with the spring onions.

Garlic soup

Recipes for garlic soup are found throughout Spain and southern France. This version comes from the central plateau in Spain where I first consumed a large bowlful, piping hot, when a friend and I arrived at the *posada* in Avila after driving through a blizzard. On the rest of that chilly trip we had garlic soup every day for lunch.

serves 4

10 cloves garlic, crushed

3 tablespoons fruity olive oil

salt and freshly ground black pepper

2 egg yolks

4 slices day-old fairly dense bread

Put 1 litre of water, the garlic and olive oil into a pan, season and bring to the boil. Simmer for 10 minutes. Whisk the egg yolks lightly in a soup tureen and pour over the hot but not boiling soup, or serve the soup in individual bowls and stir some of the egg into each one. Add the bread to the soup and eat.

Roast parsnip and chestnut soup

Roasting brings out the nuttiness of parsnips and the sweetness of garlic. These flavours combine with the creamy texture of the chestnuts to give the soup a full, rich taste. The crisp ginger garnish adds a tangy note and a slight bite.

serves 4–6

3 large parsnips, cut into chunks

6 cloves garlic, unpeeled

3 tablespoons olive oil

1 onion, chopped

1 carrot, chopped

1 stick celery, strings removed and
   sliced

1 teaspoon garam masala or
   curry powder

250g cooked chestnuts, broken
   into pieces (see page 108)

salt and freshly ground black pepper

1.25 litres hot vegetable or
   chicken stock

2 pieces ginger, each 5–6cm long

2 tablespoons sunflower oil

Preheat the oven to 200°C/400°F/gas mark 6. Arrange the parsnips and garlic on a baking tray, drizzle with half the olive oil and roast for 30 minutes, or until the vegetables are soft. Meanwhile, heat the remaining oil in a large pan and gently fry the onion, carrot and celery. Add the garam masala or curry powder and stir until its aroma is released, then add the roasted parsnips, the cloves of garlic (slipped out of their skins) and chestnuts. Season, add the hot stock and simmer for 25–30 minutes, then blend the soup and pour into individual bowls.

For the garnish, cut the ginger into julienne strips, heat the sunflower oil in a small frying pan until very hot and fry the ginger quickly, turning it and shaking the pan so that it becomes crisp, about a minute. Sprinkle on top of each bowl of soup and serve.

Spiced pumpkin soup

This is fast to make once you've cleaned the pumpkin. Pumpkin's mild, sweet taste combines well with coconut milk and both are enhanced by spices. In this soup, the citrus flavours of lemongrass and ground coriander set off the bite of ginger and chillies, with a background note of earthy turmeric.

serves 4–6

2 tablespoons sunflower oil

½ teaspoon ground coriander

½ teaspoon ground fennel seeds

1 teaspoon turmeric

1 large onion, chopped

2cm ginger, chopped

2 cloves garlic, chopped

1kg pumpkin, peeled and cubed

2 dried chillies

2 stalks lemongrass, bruised

salt, to taste

600ml vegetable stock

400ml coconut milk

lime juice (optional)

Heat the oil in a large heavy pan and fry the coriander, fennel and turmeric until their aromas are released. Stir in the onion, ginger and garlic and fry for 3–4 minutes more, then add the pumpkin, chillies and lemongrass. Stir well, season with a little salt and pour over the stock. Cover the pan and simmer until the pumpkin softens, then stir in the coconut milk. Do not cover the pan now or the coconut milk may curdle.

Bring the soup back to a simmer and cook until the pumpkin is soft enough to crush with a wooden spoon. Discard the chillies and lemongrass and blend the soup. Taste and if you wish to sharpen the flavour, stir in a little lime juice. Sieve the soup and serve with bread.

Jerusalem artichoke soup

Jerusalem artichokes are an underrated vegetable, perhaps because some people suffer wind problems from eating them. Long, slow cooking helps reduce that problem. This delicately flavoured, pale soup is one of the best winter soups I know. As you peel the artichokes drop them into water acidulated with a little lemon juice or vinegar to prevent them discolouring.

serves 4–6

80g butter

1 onion, chopped

750g Jerusalem artichokes, peeled
   and thickly sliced

1 litre vegetable or chicken stock,
   or water

salt and freshly ground black pepper

pinch of nutmeg

200ml single cream

2 dried horn of plenty mushrooms
   per serving, crumbled, to garnish

Heat 60g of the butter in a large pan and sweat the onion and artichokes, with the lid on, over a low heat for 8–10 minutes, stirring frequently. Do not let them brown. Add the stock or water and season with salt, pepper and nutmeg. Bring to the boil and simmer for 20–25 minutes until the vegetables are soft. Blend the soup, stir in the cream and reheat gently. Whisk in the remaining butter and serve at once, garnished with the horns of plenty.

Spinach bouillabaisse

We are familiar, if only in name, with the fish bouillabaisse of Marseilles, but this equally traditional, rustic dish is little known. It is marvellously cheering in miserable weather.

serves 4–6

1kg spinach, thick stalks discarded

50ml olive oil, plus extra for
   the bread

1 onion, chopped

500g waxy potatoes, sliced
   5mm thick

salt and freshly ground black pepper

a few saffron threads, crushed and
   dissolved in a little water

1 litre hot chicken or vegetable
   stock, or water

2 cloves garlic, chopped

1 bouquet garni

4–6 slices bread

4–6 eggs

Plunge the spinach into boiling water and cook for 5 minutes. Drain well, squeezing out all the moisture with your hands, and chop. Heat the oil in a large pan and sauté the onion for 1 minute, without letting it brown. Add the spinach and turn it in the oil for 5 minutes over a low heat. Put in the potatoes, season with salt and pepper and the saffron and pour over the hot stock or water. Add the garlic and bouquet garni, cover the pan and simmer over a low heat until the potatoes are cooked.

When they are ready, remove and discard the bouquet garni. Meanwhile, heat a little oil in a frying pan and lightly fry a slice of bread per person on both sides. Break 1 egg per person separately into the soup and let them poach; it will take 3–4 minutes at the most. To serve the bouillabaisse, put a slice of fried bread in each soup plate, place a poached egg on top and pour over a ladleful of the soup.

Iranian onion soup

The flavours of turmeric and fenugreek in this peasant soup make it richly warming. The turmeric adds depth and a pale golden colour and the fenugreek a savoury aroma that combines well with the mellowness of the onions. Dried fenugreek leaves can be bought from Indian and Iranian shops and from some on-line spice merchants.

serves 4–6

4 medium to large onions, halved
   and thinly sliced
4 tablespoons sunflower oil
2 tablespoons plain flour
1 tablespoon dried fenugreek
   leaves
1 teaspoon turmeric
salt, to taste
1.5 litres vegetable stock or water
juice of 3 lemons or 4 limes
$^{1}/_{2}$ teaspoon ground cinnamon
sugar (optional)
2 eggs
1 teaspoon crushed dried mint,
   to garnish
yogurt, to serve (optional)

Fry the onions gently in 3 tablespoons of the oil for 10–15 minutes until golden brown. Stir in the flour, fenugreek, turmeric and a little salt. Keep stirring as you add the stock or water and the lemon or lime juice. Cover the pan, bring the liquid to the boil, then lower the heat and simmer for 1 hour.

Stir in the cinnamon, taste the soup, and add a little sugar if it is too sour. Whisk the eggs lightly, remove the pan from the heat and pour the eggs into the soup, stirring constantly.

Pour the soup into individual bowls. Heat the remaining oil in a small pan, stir in the mint. and add a little to each bowl. Serve with bread and a bowl of yogurt, if you wish.

Yogurt soup

This Turkish soup of yogurt and rice, flavoured with mint, is a staple of the Anatolian plateau. Its Turkish name, *yayla çorbasi*, means plateau soup. I have eaten it there in bitter mid-winter and it certainly revives body and spirit. Turks never eat anything without lots of bread, and this soup is no exception, so put a basket of warmed Turkish flatbread on the table as well and you have a satisfying simple meal.

The soup can be made with meat or chicken stock or with water. Yogurt has to be stabilised before being heated or it will curdle. This is done by whisking a flour and water paste and/or an egg into the yogurt before heating it.

serves 6

60g rice

750ml stock or water

300ml yogurt

3 tablespoons plain flour mixed
    with 2 tablespoons water

1 egg

salt, to taste

50g butter

2 tablespoons crushed dried mint

chilli flakes, to garnish

Put the rice and stock or water into a large pan, bring to the boil and simmer until the rice is tender, about 25 minutes. Put the yogurt into a large bowl and whisk in the flour paste and egg. Add a ladleful of the hot stock, and stir to blend thoroughly. Pour the yogurt mixture into the pan, stirring all the time. Season with a little salt and simmer over a low heat for 10 minutes.

Melt the butter in a frying pan, add the crushed mint and sauté for 1–2 minutes. Pour this into the soup and garnish with a sprinkling of chilli flakes over the top.

salads & light dishes

Figs with mozzarella and mint

Figs are available until December and this simple Italian salad makes an excellent first course. The figs must be perfectly ripe and buy the best buffalo mozzarella.

serves 6

8 large ripe figs, thinly sliced

300–350g buffalo mozzarella, thinly sliced

1–2 tablespoons balsamic vinegar

2–3 tablespoons extra virgin olive oil

salt and freshly ground black pepper

5–6 young mint sprigs, leaves picked

Arrange the figs and the mozzarella in alternate slices on a serving platter. Whisk together the vinegar and oil and season with a little salt. Spoon the dressing over the salad, grind over some black pepper and garnish with the mint leaves.

Variation

Take 2 figs and about 30g feta per person. Cut the figs into quarters and the feta into dice. Arrange them on a platter. Omit salt from the dressing because feta is salty, and replace the balsamic vinegar with a little lemon juice. Garnish with walnuts and, if you happen to have some, pomegranate seeds.

Watercress, citrus and tuna salad

The idea for this salad came from one of England's greatest cooks, Robert May, who advocated a salad of watercress, orange and lemon dressed with oil and vinegar in his *The Accomplisht Cook*, published in 1660.

serves 4

2 oranges, peeled and pith removed

1 lemon, peeled and pith removed

2 bunches watercress, large stalks removed

200g tinned tuna, drained and broken into chunks

½ small red onion, finely sliced

4 tablespoons olive oil

salt and freshly ground black pepper

Cut the oranges and lemon into segments over a bowl so that you catch all the juices and discard the pips. Arrange the watercress on a platter, add the fruit segments and tuna. Scatter over slivers of onion, then make a dressing with the citrus juices, oil and salt and pepper. Taste to see that the balance is right. Spoon this over the salad and serve.

Variation

Add a few sliced radishes, if you wish.

Red peppers with olives and anchovies

A mixture of black, purple and dark green bruised-looking olives will add variety of flavour and colour to this Italian salad.

serves 4

4 red peppers

large handful parsley leaves

4 tablespoons extra virgin olive oil

2 tablespoons red wine vinegar

freshly ground black pepper

100g olives

8 tinned anchovy fillets

Roast the peppers (see page 44), then peel, core and seed them and cut the flesh into strips. Chop the parsley coarsely, reserving some whole leaves for the garnish. Whisk together the oil and vinegar with some black pepper. Put the peppers, chopped parsley and olives into a bowl and toss with the dressing. Arrange the anchovies and whole parsley leaves on top and serve.

Moroccan carrot salad

Morocco has more, and more varied, carrot salads than any other country I am aware of. This one is perfect for winter.

serves 4–6

500g carrots, left whole

1 clove garlic, peeled

1 teaspoon ground cumin

1 teaspoon paprika

1/2 teaspoon ground cinnamon

1/2 teaspoon sugar

pinch of salt

3 tablespoons lemon juice

1 tablespoon sunflower oil

1 tablespoon chopped parsley, to garnish

Cook the carrots in boiling salted water with the garlic until tender, then drain and dice them. Discard the garlic. Combine the spices, sugar and salt with the lemon juice. Whisk in the oil and coat the carrots with the dressing. Garnish with the parsley when the carrots are cold.

Avocado, pomegranate and wild rocket salad

The deep red pomegranate seeds give this salad a bright note on a wintry day and their sweet juiciness contrasts well with the peppery rocket, the smoothness of the avocado and the crunchy cucumber.

serves 4

3 tablespoons extra virgin olive oil
   or avocado oil
2 tablespoons sherry vinegar
salt and freshly ground black pepper
1 shallot, finely chopped
½ cucumber
1 pomegranate
1 large avocado
squeeze of lemon juice
2–3 large handfuls wild rocket

Make a dressing with the oil, vinegar, salt and pepper and add the shallot when you are ready to prepare the salad. Cut the cucumber in 4 lengthways, remove the seeds and cut each quarter into 2 strips. Cut the strips into dice, put them in a colander and sprinkle with salt.

Cut the top from the pomegranate and pull it apart gently. Pick out the seeds and discard all the pith. Put the seeds and any juice into a bowl. Dice the avocado and sprinkle with lemon juice to prevent the flesh discolouring. Rinse the cucumber and dry on a clean tea towel.

To assemble, put the rocket into a salad bowl, scatter over the cucumber and avocado and finally the pomegranate seeds. Add pomegranate juice to the dressing if you wish. Whisk the dressing and pour it over the salad.

Variation
Omit the shallot from the dressing and replace the cucumber with 60g of toasted and skinned hazelnuts or toasted pine nuts.

Butternut and green bean salad

This salad came about from having a piece of squash, a head of frisée and some green beans in the fridge, and being brought a large bag of pumpkin seeds. It has become a regular winter salad in our household. If you wish, you can add a roasted and peeled red pepper, cut into squares.

serves 4

600g butternut squash, peeled,
   seeded and cubed
6 tablespoons olive oil
200g green beans
50g pumpkin seeds
2 tablespoons lemon or lime juice
1 teaspoon Dijon mustard
salt and freshly ground black pepper
large handful frisée leaves or
   2 heads chicory

Preheat the oven to 200°C/400°F/gas mark 6. Toss the squash with 2 tablespoons of oil and roast, turning occasionally, for about 30 minutes until soft and golden. Boil the beans in salted water until just tender. Drain and rinse under cold water. Toast the pumpkin seeds in a dry frying pan, shaking from time to time so that they don't burn. Tip them into a bowl.

Whisk the lemon juice and mustard together, season with a little salt and a good grinding of pepper and whisk in the remaining oil. If you are using chicory, cut off the base and separate the leaves. Toss the frisée or chicory leaves lightly in the dressing and arrange on a platter. Arrange the squash and beans on the leaves, spoon a little of the dressing over the vegetables, scatter over the pumpkin seeds and serve.

Celeriac in olive oil

This is a very successful Turkish way of cooking all kinds of vegetables – carrots, leeks, green beans, artichokes – to be eaten at room temperature. The vegetables are cooked slowly in olive oil and water, leaving a rich sauce as the water evaporates. It is a particularly good way of preparing celeriac.

serves 4

600g celeriac, peeled and cubed
lemon juice
80ml extra virgin olive oil
1 onion, roughly chopped
6 cloves garlic, peeled
salt
1½ teaspoons sugar
1 carrot, diced
1 potato, diced
4 tablespoons chopped dill
   or parsley
lemon wedges, to serve

Drop the celeriac into water acidulated with lemon juice to prevent discolouration. Heat the oil in a large pan and cook the onion and garlic cloves for a few minutes until soft. Add the celeriac and cook for 2–3 minutes more. Pour over 200ml of water, add salt to taste and the sugar. Bring to the boil, then reduce the heat, cover and cook for 10 minutes. Add the carrot and potato and simmer for a further 20–30 minutes until all the vegetables are tender and the liquid considerably reduced. Stir in the dill or parsley and leave to cool. Serve at room temperature with lemon wedges.

The celeriac goes well with almost any of the other vegetable salads – Moroccan Carrot Salad (see page 25), Butternut and Green Bean Salad (see opposite) or Red Peppers with Olives and Anchovies (see page 25).

Aubergine kookoo

Iranian kookoos are substantial omelettes, something like a Spanish tortilla, and can be made with a variety of vegetables. With bread and a dollop of thick yogurt and some fresh herbs, they make a good first course or light meal. If any is left over, the kookoo is good cold, too.

serves 4–6

4 medium aubergines, peeled
  and cubed
4 tablespoons olive oil
2 onions, chopped
3 cloves garlic, chopped
1 teaspoon baking powder
1 tablespoon plain flour
salt and freshly ground black pepper
3 tablespoons lemon or lime juice
6 eggs
thick yogurt and fresh herbs,
  to serve

Put the aubergine into a large pan of boiling water. Simmer for 10–12 minutes until soft, then drain thoroughly. Heat half the oil in a pan and fry the onions until softened and lightly coloured. Add the garlic and fry for a minute more. Remove the onions and garlic from the pan and set aside.

Preheat the oven to 180°C/350°F/gas mark 4. Put the aubergine, baking powder, flour, seasoning and lemon juice into a food processor and blend to a coarse purée. Whisk the eggs in a large bowl, then stir in the aubergine mixture and the onion and garlic. Brush a 20cm ovenproof dish with the remaining oil, pour in the mixture and bake for 45–50 minutes until the kookoo has a deep golden colour. Cut in wedges and serve with a bowl of yogurt and a bowl of mint, coriander, basil and other herb sprigs.

Variation

If you prefer, the kookoo can be cooked in a frying pan; heat the oil, pour in the mixture and cook, covered, over a low heat for about 25 minutes. Turn the kookoo and cook on the other side for a further 10–15 minutes.

Grilled sliced aubergines with walnuts

Grilled aubergines are simple and quick to prepare and can be topped with a variety of mixtures and sauces. In addition to the suggestions in the recipe, try coriander leaves, green chilli and ginger all chopped into thick plain yogurt, or grilled, chopped red pepper mixed with chopped anchovy, parsley and black olives. Tomato or red pepper chutney is another possibility.

serves 4

2 large aubergines, peeled and cut
   into 1cm-thick slices

3 tablespoons olive oil

¼ teaspoon ground chilli

1 tablespoon red wine vinegar

3 tablespoons pomegranate
   molasses (see page 95)

salt

80g walnuts, finely chopped

Heat the grill or a griddle plate. Brush the aubergines with olive oil and grill until softened and lightly browned, about 4–5 minutes each side. Stir the chilli and vinegar into the molasses, season with a little salt if necessary and mix in the walnuts. Arrange the aubergine slices on a platter, spoon the walnut and pomegranate mixture onto each one and serve as a first course or as part of a meal of small dishes.

Variation

For grilled aubergine slices with ricotta, pine nuts and mint, crumble 100g of ricotta and mix with 3 tablespoons of toasted pine nuts and 2 tablespoons of chopped mint. Use as a topping for the aubergine slices.

Hot-sour prawn salad

This quickly made salad, drawing on the flavours of Southeast Asia, makes a fresh-tasting first course in winter.

serves 4–6

3 tablespoons lime juice

2 teaspoons fish sauce

2 tablespoons sunflower oil

500g medium or large cooked
   prawns, shelled

I shallot, finely chopped

I green chilli, seeded and finely
   chopped

lower part of I stalk lemongrass,
   finely sliced

2 tablespoons chopped coriander

2–3 handfuls lamb's lettuce,
   watercress or rocket

mint leaves, to garnish

Whisk together the lime juice, fish sauce and sunflower oil and dress the prawns. Add the shallot, chilli, lemongrass and coriander and toss through. Arrange the salad leaves in a shallow bowl, top with the prawns and dressing and garnish with mint leaves.

Variation

For a more substantial salad, add 80–100g of cellophane noodles. Soak them in hot water for 10 minutes, drain, rinse in cold water and cut into short lengths using scissors. Stir in the noodles when you add the shallot and other flavourings. If necessary, make a little more dressing.

Seafood salad

The ingredients list for this salad looks daunting, and some time is needed to prepare the fish, but then the cooking is quick and easy. It is a spectacular dish to make for a large gathering, whether as a first course for dinner or a central platter for a cold meal. The combination of seafood given here is a suggestion; buy what looks best at the fishmongers. Use 2 or 3 different fish: sea bass, salmon, monkfish and sole are all suitable. Clams could replace the mussels; baby octopus the squid.

serves 8–10

300g thin green beans, trimmed

I tablespoon olive oil

Ikg mussels

sprig of thyme

Cook the beans until just tender. Rinse under cold water, drain, toss in olive oil and put aside. Scrub the mussels, remove the beards and discard any with broken shells or that remain open when tapped. Put the mussels in a large pan over a high heat with the thyme, bay leaf and wine and cover. Shake the pan a few times and when the mussels open, scoop them into a

1 bay leaf

150ml white wine or water

500g firm fish fillet, cut into strips diagonally

500g medium raw prawns

10 large scallops, cleaned and roes removed

500g small squid, cleaned

2 heads fennel, trimmed, sliced vertically and cut into strips

2 tablespoons chopped dill, to garnish

for the sauce

1/2 teaspoon powdered saffron

salt and freshly ground black pepper

juice of 1 large lemon

180ml crème fraîche

colander standing in a bowl to catch the cooking liquor. Discard any mussels that have not opened, remove the rest from their shells and put them in a small bowl along with a little of the liquor to keep them moist. Strain all the remaining cooking liquid through a sieve lined with damp muslin.

Reheat the mussel stock and poach the fish fillets until opaque; 2–4 minutes, depending on the fish. Lift out the pieces with a slotted spoon and leave to one side. Allow the stock to cool. Bring a pan of salted water to the boil and cook the prawns until they turn pink but remain firm. Drain and plunge them into iced water, then drain and shell them and set aside.

Cut the scallops in half horizontally, put them in a pan which just holds them side by side and pour over the cooled mussel stock. Heat gently until the stock almost comes to the boil. Take the pan off the heat and leave until the scallops are opaque and firm, about 1 minute. Remove them with a slotted spoon and set aside.

Cut the squid into thin rings and split the tentacles in two at the base. Bring the mussel stock to a rolling boil. Add the squid pieces, stir and swirl around and just before the liquid returns to the boil, tip them into a colander standing in a bowl to catch the stock. Put the squid aside.

To make the sauce, return the stock to the pan and reduce to 4 tablespoons over a moderate heat. Stir in the saffron and leave to cool. Taste (it will probably be quite salty), season with pepper and stir in half the lemon juice. Add the crème fraîche, taste and add more lemon juice or seasoning if needed.

To serve, arrange the beans and fennel on a platter. Drain the mussels, put them in a bowl with the squid, spoon over about half the sauce, stir gently to coat them, then arrange on the vegetables. Add the fish and scallops to the sauce remaining in the bowl and coat them carefully. Lift them out and set them on the platter. Add a little more sauce to the bowl if necessary, toss the prawns in it and put them on the salad. Spoon over the remaining sauce and sprinkle with dill.

Oysters with spinach and saffron sauce

'A loaf of bread,' the Walrus said,
'Is chiefly what we need;
Pepper and vinegar besides
Are very good indeed –
Now if you're ready, Oysters dear,
We can begin to feed.'

Lewis Carroll, 'The Walrus and the Carpenter' from *Through the Looking-Glass*

Oysters are at their best in the winter months, and if you tire of eating them fresh, try this lightly grilled dish.

serves 4

large pinch of saffron threads

24 oysters

120g spinach, thick stalks removed

20g butter

freshly ground black pepper

squeeze of lemon juice

coarse salt

120ml dry vermouth

100ml double cream

1 egg yolk

Crumble the saffron threads and soak in 2–3 tablespoons of hot water. Open the oysters, making sure to sever the oyster from the muscle that attaches it to the shell. Reserve the deep shells and strain the liquor into a bowl. (You don't need it for this dish, but it is too good to waste. Freeze it and use in a fish soup.) Blanch the spinach leaves, drain them well and chop. Melt the butter in a frying pan and cook the spinach gently for a few minutes. Season with pepper and lemon juice.

Sprinkle a good layer of coarse salt onto a grill or baking tray for the oysters to sit in. Put a little spinach and an oyster into each shell and place them on the salt. You may have to work in batches. Meanwhile, heat the vermouth and saffron in a small pan and reduce by half. Whisk the cream and egg yolk together lightly and pour into the vermouth. Cook gently, without boiling, until the sauce thickens enough to coat the oysters.

Heat the grill. Spoon the sauce over the oysters and put them under the grill for 1–2 minutes to brown the surface lightly. Serve at once.

Chicken with sweet chilli sauce

Steeping is a standard Chinese way of cooking chicken, whether a whole bird, or pieces as here. It takes no time at all and produces tender, juicy chicken. Other vegetables can replace the broccolini, such as thin green beans or sugar snap peas, or the traditional Chinese accompaniment of cucumber.

aserves 4

500g skinned chicken breasts
   (choose large ones)
2 slices ginger, lightly crushed
1 small spring onion, chopped and
   lightly crushed
5–6 Sichuan peppercorns
250g broccolini, trimmed
1 teaspoon sesame oil

for the sauce
6 tablespoons sugar
4 medium red chillies, seeded and
   finely sliced
2 cloves garlic, finely chopped
small piece of ginger, cut into
   matchsticks
5 tablespoons rice or cider vinegar
1 tablespoon fish sauce
3 tablespoons chopped coriander
salt and freshly ground black pepper

Take a small heavy-based pan that will fit the chicken snugly and add enough water to cover it by 2cm. Before adding the chicken, add the ginger, spring onions and Sichuan peppercorns to the pan, cover and bring the water to the boil over a high heat. Add the chicken, pushing it under the surface of the water, then cover once more, remove from the heat and leave for at least 1 hour.

Blanch the broccolini in boiling water for 3 minutes, drain, refresh with cold running water and drain again, then set aside. To make the sauce, heat 120ml of water together with the sugar to make a syrup. Simmer for a few minutes and when it starts to thicken stir in all the ingredients except the coriander. Bring to the boil and simmer for 3 minutes. Pour the sauce into a bowl and leave to cool, then stir in the coriander. Taste for seasoning; I find the fish sauce makes it salty enough, but add salt if you wish.

To assemble the dish, lift the chicken from the liquid (the liquid can be strained, refrigerated and used as a light stock) and slice thinly on the diagonal against the grain. Toss the broccolini in the sesame oil and arrange on a platter. Place the chicken on top, spoon over a little of the sauce and serve the rest separately.

Spinach and chicken liver salad

Chicken livers and spinach with a balsamic vinaigrette make a mellow-tasting salad. But it is a salad capable of variation: curly endive or escarole can replace spinach; grilled bits of bacon or lardons or slices of chorizo can replace the chicken livers with the oil from cooking them used in the dressing. Poached or chopped hard-boiled eggs are a good addition to any version.

serves 4

150g day-old bread, crusts removed

6 tablespoons olive oil

250g chicken livers

50g butter

500g baby spinach leaves

salt and freshly ground black pepper

3 tablespoons balsamic vinegar

Preheat the oven to 170°C/325°F/gas mark 3. Tear the bread into chunks and pulse in a food processor to reduce to large crumbs. Spread these on a baking sheet and sprinkle over 2 tablespoons of the olive oil. Bake in the oven for few minutes until golden, then transfer to a bowl.

Trim the chicken livers, discarding any green or stringy bits, and cut them in half. Heat the butter in a frying pan and cook the livers gently until browned on the outside, but still pink inside. Meanwhile, put the spinach leaves in a salad bowl, season and toss in the remaining olive oil.

Scatter over the breadcrumbs and arrange the livers on top. Return the pan to the heat, stir in the vinegar, scraping up any bits stuck to the pan and pour this over the salad.

Grape pickers' potatoes

This dish, traditional to the grape pickers of Burgundy, is remarkable for its simplicity, its visual appeal and its fine flavour. I have to admit to changing it slightly; the original dish has slices of lightly salted pork put into the layers, but I find the bacon surrounding the potatoes provides enough meat, and instead use a little more cheese. In the unlikely event that you have any of the dish left over, it tastes good cold.

serves 4

30g butter, plus extra melted
    butter for brushing
300g thin smoked streaky
    bacon rashers
600g potatoes, peeled and
    thinly sliced
freshly ground black pepper
120g Gruyère or similar
    cheese, grated

Preheat the oven to 220°C/425°F/gas mark 7. Brush a 24–26cm cast-iron or similarly heavy ovenproof dish with a little melted butter. Line the dish with the rashers of bacon, covering the bottom and sides and leaving the upper third or so of each rasher hanging over the top of the dish. Put in a layer of potatoes, season with pepper and scatter over some cheese. Repeat the layers, finishing with potatoes. Cover the potatoes with the overhanging bacon and dot with the butter. Cover with a double layer of foil and bake for about 1 hour until the potatoes are cooked.

Remove the dish from the oven, uncover and let it stand for 5 minutes. Loosen the bacon rashers from the sides of the dish and turn the 'cake' out onto a warm serving dish. A green salad is a good accompaniment.

Wrinkled potatoes with mojo

Papas Arrugadas con Mojo is a traditional dish of the Canaries, harking back to early contacts with the foods of the New World; the new ingredients reached there before they reached the mainland. Potatoes are called 'papas' as in the Americas, not 'patatas' as in Spain, and the term 'mojo' means marinade or sauce in the New World, but not in Spain. Mojos are spicy sauces found in the Canary Islands where they are served to accompany this dish of 'wrinkled' potatoes. Covered with a layer of oil in a closed jar, the mojo will keep for up to 2 weeks in the refrigerator.

It is a decidedly moreish winter evening dish, especially if eaten by a large group sitting around the kitchen table. If you eat enough of it, and it is easy to do that, all you need afterwards is a large salad.

serves 4

500g small potatoes, left unpeeled

100g coarse salt (table salt will
    not do)

for the green mojo

1 sweet green pepper, seeded and
    roughly chopped

2 green chillies, seeded and
    roughly chopped

4–8 cloves garlic, crushed with a
    little salt

1 teaspoon ground cumin

large bunch of parsley, leaves
    picked

2 tablespoons white wine vinegar

6 tablespoons olive oil

Put the potatoes in a pan and almost cover with cold water. Add the salt, bring to the boil and reduce the heat so that the potatoes cook slowly – about 15 minutes. Meanwhile, prepare the mojo. Pound the vegetables, cumin and parsley in a mortar, adding vinegar and oil a little at a time, or blend all in a blender or food processor.

Test the potatoes with a skewer to see if they are done. Drain off the water, keep the potatoes in the pan and shake over a low heat so that the potatoes are wrinkled and finely coated with salt on the outside, soft and tender inside. Serve with the mojo.

Georgian cheese bread

My only visit to Georgia was in bleak mid-winter a few years ago. Tbilisi was full of refugees from fighting in the Black Sea provinces. It was bitterly cold, the economy was on the point of collapse and there was a fuel crisis. Electricity was on only a few hours a day and shops had their own tiny generators. People wore several layers of clothing and remained resolutely cheerful, helpful, proud of their country and their beautiful city and determined that a foreigner should experience it to the full. I was taken around the city and the countryside nearby; I had simple family meals, was guest of honour at a memorable Georgian feast with its ritual toasting, and walked the streets of Tbilisi eating khachapuri – the marvellous, sustaining cheese bread that is the closest Georgians come to fast food.

Many types of dough are used for khachapuri; commercial bakers use a yeast dough that is very filling; a rich version is made with a buttery dough that resembles flaky pastry. This recipe uses the yogurt dough most often used in Georgian homes. The salted white cheese, most commonly used for the filling, is first soaked in water. I find a mixture of feta and slightly sour, crumbly cheeses such as Wensleydale, white Cheshire or Lancashire is good.

serves 8

3 eggs

175ml yogurt

200g plain white flour, plus extra
    for dusting

½ teaspoon salt

½ teaspoon bicarbonate of soda

50g cold butter, cut into pieces,
    plus extra for greasing

450g cheese (see above)

Preheat the oven to 180°C/350°F/gas mark 4. Beat 1 egg in a large bowl and stir in the yogurt. Mix together the flour, salt and bicarbonate of soda in another bowl and rub in the butter until the mixture resembles fine breadcrumbs. Add the flour mixture to the yogurt and stir to form a dough. Add a little more flour if it is too soft. Knead into a smooth elastic dough and leave to rest while you prepare the cheese.

Grate or crumble the cheeses coarsely. Beat the second egg and stir it into the cheese. Set aside. Divide the dough into 8 pieces, roll each one on a floured board to a circle of about 12–14cm diameter and put one eighth of the cheese mixture in the centre. Gather up the sides to meet in the centre and either crimp the edges together to enclose the cheese completely, or leave them slightly open. Put the breads onto a large, greased baking sheet. Brush with the third beaten egg and bake for 25–30 minutes until browned. The bread is best served hot or warm. Serve it as a satisfying first course or with a salad as a light meal.

Variation

If you prefer to make 1 large khachapuri, roll out the dough into a large oblong. Cover one half with cheese, fold over the other half to enclose it, crimp the edges to seal, brush with egg and bake for about 40–45 minutes.

Gratin of spinach and snails

A fast, simple dish that will serve two as a light meal or four as a first course. Most delicatessens sell cans of snails.

serves 2–4

1.2kg fresh spinach, large stalks
    removed, or 600g frozen
60g butter
3 cloves garlic, finely chopped
24 snails
salt and freshly ground black pepper
good pinch of nutmeg
200ml crème fraîche
dried breadcrumbs and grated
    Parmesan, for sprinkling

Cook the fresh spinach in boiling water for a few minutes, refresh it under cold running water, squeeze it well and chop it. If using frozen spinach, follow the instructions on the packet and chop it if necessary.

Preheat the oven to 180°C/350°F/gas mark 4. Melt 15g of the butter in a small pan, add 1 clove of garlic and when it begins to sizzle, add the snails. If they are very large you may want to cut them in half. Cook for a minute, turning the snails in the garlic butter. Cover with a lid, then remove the pan from the heat and set aside.

Butter a large gratin dish, then put half of the remaining butter into a large pan and add the rest of the garlic. When it starts to colour add the spinach. Stir it well for about 5 minutes, seasoning with pepper and nutmeg and lightly with salt. Add the crème fraîche, a little at a time, until the spinach has absorbed it all. Turn the spinach into the gratin dish, poke holes in the surface and put a snail in each. If any of the butter and garlic remains in the snail pan pour it over the spinach. Smooth over the surface and sprinkle generously with breadcrumbs and grated Parmesan. Dot with the remaining butter and bake in the oven for 20–25 minutes until the surface is golden.

Shallot tarte tatin

Peeling a kilo of shallots is time-consuming, but once that is done the tart is quickly assembled and is invariably a great success.

serves 4–6

for the shortcrust pastry
200g plain flour, plus extra
   for dusting
1/4 teaspoon salt
100g butter, cut into small pieces
1 egg yolk, lightly beaten (optional)
3–4 tablespoons iced water
   (more if needed)

for the filling
1kg shallots, peeled (and halved
   if very large)
60g butter
3 tablespoons sunflower oil
180ml Marsala or sweet sherry
2 tablespoons sugar
salt and freshly ground black pepper

Make the shortcrust pastry following the method on page 184 but omitting the sugar. Preheat the oven to 180°C/350°F/gas mark 4. Put the shallots on a roasting tray, dot with half the butter and sprinkle over the oil, Marsala and sugar. Roast the shallots in the oven for about 30 minutes, stirring from time to time to make sure they do not caramelise too much. Remove the shallots from the oven and season with salt and pepper.

Use the remaining butter to coat the base of a 26cm fixed-base tart tin. Turn the shallots and their juices into the tin, spreading them evenly over the base. Roll out the pastry in a circle slightly larger than the tin, lift it over the shallots and tuck the edges inside the tin. Put the tart into the oven and bake for about 45 minutes. The pastry should be nicely browned and thick juices should be bubbling around the edges. If it is browning too quickly cover with a piece of foil. To serve, loosen the edges, put a large plate with a rim over the tart tin and turn upside down.

Leek and red pepper tart

This tart makes a good lunch or supper dish after a bowl of soup or before cheese and salad.

serves 4

for the shortcrust pastry
200g plain flour, plus extra
   for dusting
¼ teaspoon salt
100g butter, cut into small pieces
1 egg yolk, lightly beaten (optional)
3–4 tablespoons iced water
   (more if needed)

for the filling
2 red peppers
30g butter
1 tablespoon olive oil
1kg leeks, cut into 2cm slices,
   discarding most of the green
2 eggs
150ml crème fraîche
salt and freshly ground black pepper

Preheat the oven to 200°C/400°F/gas mark 6. Roast the peppers in the oven or over a gas flame until charred on all sides. Put them into a covered pan and set aside for 10 minutes or so. Remove the skin, core, seeds and ribs and slice the flesh into strips.

Make the pastry following the method on page 184 but omitting the sugar. Line a 26cm tart tin with the pastry and prick with a fork. Cut a piece of greaseproof paper big enough to line the tin and leave 4cm protruding above the edge. Fit it into the pastry case, pressing it into the sides of the tin. Fill it with dried beans or raw rice. Bake for 10 minutes, lower the heat to 180°C/350°F/gas mark 4 and bake for a further 5–6 minutes. Remove the partially baked case from the oven, but leave it on at this temperature.

Heat the butter and oil in a heavy pan and cook the leeks gently, stirring occasionally, until they have softened. Spread them on the pastry and arrange strips of red pepper on top. Whisk the eggs with the crème fraîche, season and pour over the leeks and peppers. Bake for 25–30 minutes.

Small savoury pastries

Filo makes light, delicate pastries in a variety of shapes and there is an infinite choice of fillings. When working with filo, use only 1–2 sheets at a time and keep the rest under a damp cloth to prevent drying out. 250g of filo will make 24–30 little pastries; you will also need melted butter or oil for brushing.

Start with 2 sheets of filo brushed with melted butter or oil. Stack them, then cut them lengthways into 3 or 4 strips, depending on the width of the sheets. Put a teaspoon of filling about 5cm from the end nearest to you, leaving a border on each side. For parcels or rolls, fold the end over the filling, fold again and fold in the sides. Continue folding to make a parcel, or roll the remaining pastry around the filling. For triangles, bring the top of the strip diagonally over the filling to meet the long side, forming a triangle. Continue to fold in the same way until the strip is used up. Always have the seam on the bottom. When you have filled the pastries, put them onto a baking sheet and bake for 15–20 minutes at 190°C/375°F/gas mark 5. Serve warm

Roast sweet potato filling
250g roast sweet potato, mashed; 1 small onion, grated; 1/4 teaspoon ground coriander; 1/4 teaspoon ground chilli; salt and freshly ground black pepper; 1/2 egg
Mix all the ingredients together.

Green olive and nut filling
200g green olives, stoned and chopped; 80g pine nuts or chopped walnuts; 2 spring onions, chopped; 1 teaspoon tomato purée; 1/4 teaspoon chilli flakes
Mix all the ingredients together.

Feta and spinach filling
100g feta, crumbled; 250g spinach, blanched, drained and chopped; freshly ground black pepper; pinch of nutmeg; 1/2 egg
Combine the feta and spinach, season well and bind with the egg.

Chicken and herb filling
1 small chicken breast, poached and shredded; a little chopped parsley; a little chopped coriander; salt; 1/4 teaspoon sweet paprika
Mix all the ingredients together.

Tuna, capers and lemon filling
200g tinned tuna, drained and mashed; a few capers, drained, rinsed and mashed; a little chopped parsley; 2 tablespoons lemon juice; salt
Stir the capers and parsley into the tuna, season with lemon juice and salt.

main dishes

Prawns and chorizo with chickpea purée

I love the spicy, pimentón-flavoured chorizo sausages we get from Spain, and their flavour combines perfectly with both chickpeas and prawns.

serves 4

400g chickpeas, soaked overnight
  and drained

4 cloves garlic, peeled

2 bay leaves

3–4 sprigs thyme

2–3 tablespoons lemon juice

salt and freshly ground black pepper

1½–2 teaspoons ground coriander

2 tablespoons olive oil, plus extra
  for drizzling

500g chorizo, cut into small chunks

500g large raw prawns, peeled and
  heads removed

watercress, to serve

Put the chickpeas in a large pan with the garlic and herbs, cover with plenty of water, bring to the boil, then simmer for about an hour. Taste to see how chewy the chickpeas are; if they are not yet tender cook for another 15 minutes or so. Drain them, reserving the liquid, discard the herbs, and blend the chickpeas with enough of the cooking liquid to make a smooth purée. Season with lemon juice, salt, pepper and coriander. Drizzle over some olive oil and keep the purée warm.

Some large prawns have a black intestinal tract. Make an incision with the tip of a small knife along the back of the prawn and lift it out. Heat the oil in a large frying pan and fry the chorizo until crisp. Remove and keep warm. Add the prawns to the fat in the pan and stir-fry until firm and cooked through, about 3–5 minutes.

Serve the purée in soup plates with the prawns and chorizo on top. Put a bowl of watercress sprigs on the table to accompany the dish.

Monkfish and mussels in saffron sauce

The lingering, earthy aroma and flavour of saffron enhance all fish and shellfish, whether in a quickly prepared sauce as here, or in a Mediterranean fish stew, like the Suquet on page 63.

serves 4

750g monkfish, boned and all filmy grey skin removed

300g mussels, scrubbed and beards removed

200ml fish stock (see page 63)

100ml white wine

large pinch of saffron threads, crushed

3 tablespoons olive oil

2 shallots, finely chopped

leaves from 2–3 sprigs thyme, chopped

salt and freshly ground black pepper

2–3 tablespoons crème fraîche

Cut the monkfish into 5mm slices and set aside. Put the mussels in a pan with the stock, wine and saffron, then cover and simmer until the mussels open, shaking the pan from time to time. Lift out the mussels, discard any that haven't opened and strain the liquid through a very fine sieve or one lined with damp muslin. Cover the mussels and keep warm.

Heat 1 tablespoon of the oil in a small pan and cook the shallots gently until just starting to colour. Add the mussel liquor, thyme and season with pepper and a little salt. Bring to the boil and simmer to reduce by one third. Stir in the crème fraîche and keep warm.

Heat the remaining oil in a heavy frying pan and fry the monkfish on both sides for 3–4 minutes until opaque. Put the monkfish and mussels onto a warm serving platter, pour over the sauce and serve with rice.

Seared scallops with wild mushrooms

Select the wild mushrooms according to what looks best in the market – ceps, girolles, chanterelles, pieds de mouton are all suitable. You can freeze scallop roes for a short time.

serves 4

300g mixed wild mushrooms
12 large scallops, roes removed
   and kept for another dish
30g butter
2 tablespoons olive oil
chopped parsley, to garnish

Discard any dubious bits and slice the mushrooms, including the stalks. Wipe the scallops and cut them into 2 or 3 slices horizontally.

Heat the butter in a frying pan until it foams and cook the mushrooms in batches, stirring frequently until they become soft. Keep warm while you cook the scallops. Heat another frying pan, brush the scallops on both sides with a little oil and sear for 30 seconds on each side. Arrange the mushrooms on a platter, top with the scallops and garnish with chopped parsley. Serve with Provençal Lentils (see page 150).

Scallops with winter vegetables

Scallops have a delicate, sweet taste which is matched by the sweet notes in winter vegetables. I have used the vegetables I like best, but parsnips and celeriac make good partners, too.

serves 4

100g carrot
100g Jerusalem artichoke
100g fennel
1 tablespoon olive oil
50g butter
salt and freshly ground black pepper
12 large scallops
3 tablespoons white wine

Prepare the scallops as above, but keep them whole and include the roes if you wish. Cut the vegetables into matchsticks. Heat the oil and a little of the butter in a frying pan and sauté the vegetables for 3–4 minutes until softened and just starting to brown. Season and keep them warm on a serving dish.

Heat the rest of the butter in another pan, put in the scallops and sauté for 2–3 minutes. Arrange the scallops on the bed of vegetables. Deglaze the scallop pan with the white wine, pour the juices over the scallops and serve.

Grilled brill fillets with lemon and pumpkin seed salsa

Grilled fish is fast to prepare, and if you take a little more time and marinate the fish first you can easily vary the flavours of your winter suppers. I've used brill fillets for this recipe, but bream, cod or snapper would be good choices, too.

serves 2

2 brill fillets, weighing about
   200g each

3–4 tablespoons soy sauce

2 cloves garlic, finely chopped

small piece of ginger,
   finely chopped

1/4 teaspoon five spice powder
   (optional)

2 tablespoons sunflower oil

for the salsa

1 preserved lemon

70g green olives, stoned
   and chopped

2 tablespoons pumpkin seeds,
   toasted and lightly crushed

2–3 spring onions, finely chopped

2 tablespoons chopped parsley

1–2 tablespoons olive oil

Put the fillets side by side in a dish, mix together the soy sauce, garlic, ginger and five spice and spoon it over the fish to cover it evenly. Set aside for 30–60 minutes, turning the fillets once, and spooning the marinade over any bits that are still white.

Meanwhile, make the salsa. Discard the flesh of the lemon and cut the peel into dice. Combine with the olives, pumpkin seeds, spring onions and parsley and add the olive oil.

Heat the grill, remove any bits of garlic or ginger from the fish and brush on both sides with the oil. Grill for 2–3 minutes each side, depending on the thickness. Serve the fish with the salsa.

Seared bream with spinach

The family of breams is vast; they are all firm-fleshed and have a fine flavour, but the best are the gilt-head and the red bream. Fish must be fresh, and this means that it looks fresh and has no fishy smell. Look for bright eyes, deep red gills, shiny, bright skin and a firm texture.

serves 4

4 bream fillets, weighing
   180–200g each

4–5 tablespoons lemon juice

2 bay leaves

1 teaspoon dried oregano

½ teaspoon paprika

salt and freshly ground black pepper

5–6 tablespoons olive oil

750g spinach, large stalks removed

3 anchovy fillets, chopped

2 cloves garlic, chopped

Put the bream into a marinade made with 2 tablespoons of the lemon juice, the herbs, paprika, salt and pepper to taste and 1 tablespoon of the oil. Cover and set aside for an hour, turning the fish once.

While the fish is marinating, roll the spinach leaves up a few at a time into a fat cigar and cut into narrow ribbons. Heat 2 tablespoons of the oil in a large, heavy frying pan with high sides. Remove the fish from the marinade, wipe off any herbs sticking to it and sear for about 4 minutes (depending on thickness), turning the pieces once. Transfer the fish to a serving dish, cover and keep warm.

Wipe out the pan, turn the heat to low and pour in 3 tablespoons of oil. Add the anchovy and garlic, stir well so that the anchovy disintegrates and the garlic colours without burning. Pour in 2 tablespoons of lemon juice to deglaze the pan, then tip in the spinach, season with salt and pepper and stir and toss until it wilts. Sprinkle over some fresh olive oil and, if you wish, a little more lemon juice and serve with the fish.

Roast spiced tuna

A fine, thick piece of tuna can be roasted in the same manner as a beef fillet, to give a crisp outside, coated with spices, and pink flesh in the centre. In this recipe, I've used Japanese seven spice powder – shichimi togarashi – to coat the fish. This blend of white and black sesame seeds, dried tangerine peel, sansho (Japanese pepper), nori (laver), mustard seeds and chillies has a distinct citrus flavour and a pleasantly gritty texture. It is available from Japanese and other oriental shops.

aserves 4–6

5 tablespoons olive oil

800g tuna in 1 piece, about 8cm thick

2–3 tablespoons seven spice powder

Use 1 tablespoon of oil to rub the tuna on all sides, then coat it with the spice mixture. Put it in a bowl, cover and leave to marinate in the refrigerator for up to 4 hours.

Preheat the oven to 220°C/425°F/gas mark 7. Let the tuna come to room temperature, and brush a roasting dish with 1 tablespoon of oil. Heat the remaining oil in a nonstick pan and sear the fish quickly on all sides. Transfer the fish to the roasting dish and roast for 10–12 minutes, depending on its thickness. Remove the tuna from the oven, cover with foil and leave to stand for 4–5 minutes in a warm place before slicing. Serve with Swiss Chard and Potato (see page 138) or a Mash (see page 160) with Sautéed Chicory and Radicchio (see page 142).

Variation

Other spice mixtures could be used to coat the tuna, such as a simple Indian masala of coriander seed, cumin and black pepper, or a Caribbean rub of cumin, fennel seed, black pepper, chilli flakes and dried oregano. For either mixture, dry roast the cumin seeds and then grind with the other ingredients.

Tuna steaks with a balsamic vinegar glaze

This healthy fast food goes well with Braised Cavolo Nero (page 141) or Spinach with Sesame (page 138).

serves 2

2 tablespoons olive oil

60g pancetta, chopped

1 medium red onion, sliced

2 tuna steaks, weighing
 180–200g each

1 teaspoon crushed green
 peppercorns

salt

4 tablespoons white wine

2 tablespoons balsamic vinegar
 (commercial rather than
 artisan quality)

Heat 1 tablespoon of oil in a heavy frying pan and sauté the pancetta until it colours lightly and the fat runs. Add the onion and cook gently for 8–10 minutes until it is soft and lightly browned. Transfer to a serving plate and keep warm. Wipe out the pan and put in the remaining tablespoon of oil. Season the steaks on both sides with the crushed pepper and salt. Fry the steaks for 2 minutes on each side to leave them rare in the centre. Transfer the fish to the serving plate, quickly deglaze the pan with the wine and balsamic vinegar, spoon the juices over the fish and serve.

Variation
Swordfish can also be cooked in this way.

Baked sea bass with fennel and lime

A small sea bass is the perfect size for two people, and its firm flesh and fine flavour respond well to baking. Bream, John Dory or grey mullet could be used instead *(see photos overleaf)*.

serves 2

1 sea bass, weighing 500–600g

1 teaspoon fennel seeds

2 teaspoons grated unwaxed
 lime peel

½ teaspoon chilli flakes

salt

2 tablespoons olive oil

4 tablespoons lime juice

Preheat the oven to 180°C/350°F/gas mark 4. Cut 2 slits in each side of the sea bass. Mix together the fennel seeds, lime peel and chilli, with a little salt, if you wish. Push some of the spice mixture into the slits and put the rest into the cavity of the fish. Pour half of the oil into a narrow baking dish that just fits the fish, put in the fish, pour over the lime juice and the remaining oil and bake in the oven for about 25 minutes, basting occasionally. If you don't have a narrow dish, cut a large piece of foil, fold it in half, and oil the centre. Place the fish on top, fold up the sides and ends, add the lime juice and remaining oil, make into a parcel and bake on an oven tray. It will take a little longer than it does in the dish, but it won't need basting. The fish is ready when a small knife blade easily pierces the flesh near the backbone.

Poached turbot with parsley and truffle oil dressing

Apart from the time needed to make the fish stock, and that can be done in advance, this dish can be on the table in about 15 minutes. Brill, halibut steaks or skate wings are all suitable alternatives to turbot.

serves 4

1 turbot, weighing 1.3–1.5kg

salt and freshly ground black pepper

750ml fish stock made with the turbot bones (see page 63) or use ready-made

2 handfuls of parsley leaves

2 tablespoons lemon juice

2 tablespoons olive oil

1–2 tablespoons white truffle oil

Ask the fishmonger to fillet the turbot, and make sure to take the head and bones home to make the stock. Cut the fillets into 8 pieces and season them. Put the stock in a wide pan and bring to the boil. Put in the turbot, skin-side up, and simmer for about 5–6 minutes until cooked through. Lift the pieces onto a warm dish and remove the skin. Keep warm.

Put the parsley into a blender with 4–5 tablespoons of the hot stock and the lemon juice and blend to a runny purée. With the machine running, add the 2 oils through the top of the blender. Taste and season the sauce, adding more oil or lemon juice if necessary. Sieve the sauce to remove any large bits of parsley and use it at once while the flavour is fresh and the colour vivid. To serve, spoon some of the sauce onto each plate and top with 2 pieces of turbot.

Don't waste the remaining stock, strain it and use it for soup.

Variation

The dressing is very adaptable; white wine vinegar or lime juice could replace the lemon juice. If you don't like the flavour of white truffles, use walnut or hazelnut oil instead.

Cod with white beans and chorizo

The idea for this dish came from cassoulet, the classic dish of beans, duck or goose confit and other meats from southwest France. It can be made with salt cod instead of fresh, but that must be soaked for several hours before being cooked.

serves 6

500g haricot beans, soaked
   overnight and drained

1 bouquet garni

2 onions, peeled

1 clove

4 cloves garlic, peeled

3 tablespoons olive oil

400g chorizo, cut into small chunks

400g tinned chopped tomatoes

1 tablespoon tomato purée

5 tablespoons chopped parsley

salt and freshly ground black pepper

900g cod fillet, skinned and cut into
   thick slices

4 tablespoons breadcrumbs

Put the beans in a large pan with the bouquet garni, 1 onion stuck with the clove, and 2 cloves of garlic. Add 2 litres of cold water, bring to the boil, skimming the surface as necessary. Cover and simmer for about 1–1½ hours until the beans are just tender but not bursting out of their skins. Drain the beans into a bowl, reserving the cooking liquid, but discarding the other vegetables and bouquet.

Preheat the oven to 170°C/325°F/gas mark 3. Put 2 tablespoons of the oil in a frying pan, chop the remaining onion and garlic and fry until lightly browned. Add the chorizo and cook gently for 5 minutes, then add the tomatoes, tomato purée and 3 tablespoons of parsley. Season and cook over a moderate heat for 2 minutes.

Put half the beans in an earthenware casserole and cover with the tomato mixture. Put the rest of the beans on top with a small ladleful of their cooking liquid. Cover the casserole and put it into the oven for 30 minutes.

Season the cod with salt and pepper. Wipe out the pan, heat the remaining oil and cook the slices for 1–2 minutes on each side until lightly golden. Lift them out and reserve. Take the casserole from the oven, gently open up the top layer of beans and put in the pieces of fish, cover them with beans. Scatter the breadcrumbs over the top, moisten them with a little more of the cooking water and return the casserole to the oven for 8 minutes. Sprinkle over the remaining parsley and serve at once.

Octopus daube

I learned this dish from the gifted food writer Richard Olney, when visiting him one winter. We were marooned in his house, up in the hills of Provence, for several days because of a heavy snowfall. We made pasta; there were root vegetables in the cellar, a supply of cheeses and saucisson sec – and Richard had an octopus in the freezer. The freezer is a good place to keep an octopus for a short period, because freezing tenderises the flesh. If you buy a fresh one, freeze it for a couple of days and thaw in the refrigerator before using it. Many fishmongers also stock very good frozen octopus, usually from Spain, and that can be cooked once it has thawed. The daube can be prepared in advance and reheated gently the next day.

serves 6–8

1.5kg octopus (choose small ones as they are less tough)

6 tablespoons olive oil

1 large onion, chopped

4 cloves garlic, chopped

250g tomatoes, peeled, seeded and chopped, or use tinned

salt and freshly ground black pepper

1 bouquet garni of bay leaf, thyme and parsley

60ml cognac or marc

200ml white wine

100g small black olives (optional)

To clean the octopus, remove and discard the eyes, beaks and innards; there is no need to skin them. Rinse the octopus and cut them into bite-size pieces. Heat half the oil in a large frying pan and cook the onion gently until golden. Add the garlic and let it just colour. Put in the tomatoes, season and increase the heat. Simmer until the juices from the tomatoes have evaporated, and set aside.

Heat the rest of the oil in a heavy pan, put in the octopus and bouquet garni and stir and shake the pan regularly as the liquid given off by the octopus comes to the boil. Heat the cognac in a small pan, ignite it and pour it over the octopus. Shake the pan until the flames die down. Add the white wine, bring to the boil, stirring as it does so, and let it reduce slightly. Add the tomato mixture, bring back to the boil, then simmer, uncovered, for about 1–1½ hours until the octopus is tender. Stir the daube frequently while it is cooking. Just before serving stir in the black olives.

Stuffed squid

The stuffing of breadcrumbs, pine nuts and raisins comes from the Catalan coast and the Balearic islands. Sometimes the squid is simmered in saffron-flavoured stock; in winter I prefer to braise it in tomato sauce, which produces a richer dish.

serves 4

4 squid, each weighing about 200g

for the stuffing

1 small onion, finely chopped

1 tablespoon olive oil

2 cloves garlic, chopped

50g raisins

50g pine nuts

2 tablespoons finely chopped
  parsley

grated rind of 1 unwaxed lemon

4 tablespoons fresh breadcrumbs

2–3 tablespoons white wine

salt and freshly ground black pepper

pimentón (see page 118)

for the sauce

2 tablespoons olive oil

1 onion, finely chopped

2 cloves garlic, crushed

400g tinned chopped tomatoes

2 sun-dried tomatoes in oil, finely
  chopped, or 1 tablespoon
  sun-dried tomato paste

2 tablespoons chopped parsley

1 bay leaf

100ml white wine

sugar, salt and freshly ground
  black pepper

First clean the squid. Pull and twist the head to separate it from the body, removing the innards with it. Cut the tentacles from the head just above the eyes; they will remain joined together by a thin band of flesh. Within the band of flesh is the hard 'beak' which you squeeze out and discard. Discard the head and innards, hook the transparent bone out of the body with your finger and discard. Wash the tentacles and body, removing any mucus from inside the pouch. Rub the purple-red skin off with your fingers; it comes away easily. Pull off the fins and chop them finely with the tentacles.

To make the stuffing, sauté the onion in the oil until it is softened, and add the garlic and the tentacles and fins. Cook for 2–3 minutes over a low heat, then add the raisins, pine nuts, parsley, lemon rind and breadcrumbs; moisten with the wine. Season with salt, pepper and *pimentón* and mix thoroughly. Stuff the squid with the mixture and fasten the openings with wooden cocktail sticks.

To make the sauce, heat the oil in a heavy pan and sauté the onion until soft. Add the garlic and continue to cook for 2 minutes, then stir in the tomatoes, tomato paste if you are using it, the herbs and the wine. Season with a little sugar, salt and pepper. Bring the sauce to the boil. Add the squid, cover tightly and cook gently for 50–60 minutes until the squid is tender and the sauce has thickened. Serve with crusty bread.

Suquet

This fish stew comes from Catalonia and is thickened in the traditional way with a picada of toasted almonds, bread, garlic and parsley, which gives it a complex, rich flavour. I like to use two or three different fish and a few clams or mussels. Monkfish, cod, haddock, bream or sea bass are suitable, too.

serves 4

for the fish stock (makes about
    1.5 litres)
1kg white fish bones and trimmings
1 stalk celery, sliced
1 onion, chopped
1 carrot, chopped
100ml dry white wine
2 sprigs thyme
3–4 parsley stalks
1 bay leaf
10 black peppercorns

for the picada
1 slice day-old white bread
1 tablespoon olive oil
2 large cloves garlic, crushed
40g toasted almonds
a few threads of saffron
2 tablespoons chopped parsley

for the suquet
500ml fish stock (see above)
    or water
800g gurnard and hake fillets,
    cut into serving pieces
200g small clams
2 tablespoons olive oil
1 onion, chopped
2 cloves garlic, chopped
3 tomatoes, peeled and chopped
salt and freshly ground black pepper

First make the stock. Break the bones into manageable pieces and put everything into a large pan along with 1.5 litres of water. Bring to the boil and skim off any scum that rises to the surface. Simmer for 20–25 minutes. Strain and the stock is ready to use, or when cool it can be refrigerated or frozen.

To make the picada, fry the bread in the oil, remove it and lightly brown the garlic. Transfer to a food processor or use a pestle and mortar to grind them to a paste along with the almonds, saffron, parsley and a little salt. If necessary add a little stock to moisten.

Put the clams into a small pan with a little of the stock and steam until they open. Drain, reserving the stock.

Heat the oil in a heavy pan and sweat the onion gently for about 20 minutes so that it slowly caramelises. Stir in the garlic and let it start to colour, then add the tomatoes and cook until the mixture is almost dry. Add the stock, including the strained stock reserved from the clams, stir well and bring to a simmer. Season with salt and pepper. Simmer for 10 minutes to allow the flavours to blend. Add the pieces of fish and cook for about 6 minutes, depending on size and thickness. Stir in the picada, simmer for a few minutes so that the sauce thickens, then add the clams to heat through. Serve with boiled potatoes or bread.

Cacciucco

Every Italian coastal town has its zuppa di pesce or fish soup, but this one from Livorno is eaten as a main course, not as a soup. It is served over toasted slices of country bread with some of the broth, and the rest can be kept for a fish soup or a seafood risotto. Use a variety of fish and shellfish, according to what looks good when you go shopping. Don't be deterred by the long list of ingredients; there may be a lot to assemble, but the preparation is not lengthy and the dish is rich and wonderfully satisfying.

serves 8

about 2kg white fish such as gurnard, cod, haddock, hake, whiting, monkfish
300g squid, cleaned (see page 61)
6 tablespoons olive oil
6 cloves garlic, crushed
2 sticks celery, strings removed and sliced
1 onion, sliced
2 bay leaves
small bunch of parsley, chopped
400g tinned chopped tomatoes
300ml red wine
1.5 litres fish stock (see page 63) or water
1 teaspoon peperoncino or chilli flakes
salt and freshly ground black pepper
8 slices country bread
250g raw prawns in their shells
400g mussels or clams

Have the fish filleted and keep the heads and bones to make stock. Cut the fish fillets into 5cm slices. Cut the squid into rings and chop the fins and tentacles. Put them all to one side. preheat the oven to 200°C/400°F/gas mark 6.

Heat 4 tablespoons of the oil in a large, heavy pan and fry 4 cloves of garlic, the celery and onion until lightly browned, about 10 minutes. Add the bay leaves and most of the parsley, the tomatoes, wine and stock. Season with peperoncino, salt and pepper, bring to the boil and simmer gently for 45 minutes.

Meanwhile, spread the slices of bread onto a baking tray, drizzle over the remaining oil and bake for 10 minutes, or until crisp. Rub each one on both sides with the remaining garlic and set aside.

Strain the liquid into another big pan, pressing the debris to remove as much flavour as possible. Taste for seasoning; it should be spicy. Bring the liquid back to the boil and add the squid. Let it simmer gently for about 20 minutes before adding the pieces of fish. Simmer for another 4–5 minutes, then add the prawns.

Rinse out the first pan, scoop a ladleful of the simmering broth into it, add the mussels or clams, cover and cook over a high heat for about 3 minutes until they have opened. Strain through a colander standing over a bowl to catch the liquid. Strain this though a fine sieve back into the stew, discarding any gritty bits. Discard any mussels or clams that haven't opened and put the others in with the fish. Put a slice of bread into each soup plate, scoop out a sampling of fish for each serving, spoon over some of the broth and garnish with the remaining parsley.

Portuguese chicken with rice

This is a very popular Portuguese dish, and one which has many interpretations. Mine is a fairly plain version, because I like the flavours of the rice and chicken together without other intrusions, but, if you wish, you can add red or green peppers, cut into squares, mushrooms, chouriço (Portuguese spicy sausage) or flavour the rice with saffron.

serves 6

3 tablespoons olive oil

100g smoked bacon, chopped

2 medium onions, chopped

4 cloves garlic, chopped

1.5kg chicken, jointed into 6 pieces, or use thighs and drumsticks

juice of 1 lemon

salt and freshly ground black pepper

about 600ml chicken stock or water

400g long grain rice

4 cloves

2 bay leaves

chopped parsley, to garnish

Heat the oil in a large, heavy casserole, preferably earthenware, and sauté the bacon and onion until the bacon starts to brown and the onion is pale gold. Add the garlic, stir well and cook for 1–2 minutes, then put in the chicken pieces. Mix everything together gently, turning the chicken until it turns white on all sides. Squeeze over the lemon juice and season with salt and pepper.

Preheat the oven to 180°C/350°F/gas mark 4. Measure 1½ times the volume of stock or water to rice and bring it to the boil. Stir the rice into the casserole, together with the cloves and bay leaves. Pour over the stock, cover the dish with foil or a lid and transfer the casserole to the oven. Leave to cook for 1–1½ hours. Lower the heat if it seems to be cooking too quickly, add a little more stock or water if it is drying out. The rice should be moist, not bone dry. Serve from the casserole sprinkled with parsley.

Pot-roasted spiced chicken

Chicken is more usually flavoured with the warm spices of India – cumin, cardamom, cloves – but from time to time I prefer to use the refreshing citrus flavours of southeast Asia. Most of these spices are now readily available in supermarkets and oriental shops; if you can't find galangal use fresh ginger. Leave the chicken to absorb the spice flavours for a couple of hours before cooking

serves 4

2 shallots, chopped

25g galangal, chopped

4 stalks lemongrass, lower white part only, finely sliced

large handful of coriander leaves

3 tablespoons sunflower oil

salt

1 chicken, weighing about 1.5kg

6 kaffir lime leaves

4 tablespoons lime juice

Pound or process the shallots, galangal, lemongrass and coriander to a paste with 1 tablespoon of oil and a little salt. Work your fingers under the skin of the bird, carefully lifting it from the flesh without tearing it. Spread the spice mixture over the legs and breast and draw the skin back in place.

When you are ready to cook, preheat the oven to 190°C/375°F/gas mark 5. Heat the remaining oil in a heavy ovenproof casserole that is just big enough to take the chicken. Put in the lime leaves, put the chicken on its side on top of them and pour over the lime juice. Cover tightly with foil under the lid and transfer the pan to the oven. Bake for 30 minutes, turn the chicken over and cook for a further 30 minutes. Then remove the lid, turn the chicken breast upwards and bake for 10–15 minutes more.

Pierce the thickest part of the thigh with a skewer; if the juices run clear the chicken is cooked. Let it rest for 10 minutes in a warm place before carving. Discard the lime leaves and serve the chicken with the pan juices and a dish of plain or saffron-flavoured rice.

Variation

Make the same paste and rub 4 chicken pieces with it. Leave to marinate for 1 hour. Brown lightly in 1 tablespoon of oil. Pour over tamarind water made with 2 teaspoons tamarind paste and 4 tablespoons water. Cover tightly and put into the oven heated to 180°C/350°F/gas mark 4 for 20 minutes, then reduce the heat to 150°C/300°F/gas mark 2 and cook for a further 15 minutes for breasts, 20–25 minutes for legs and thighs.

Garlic chicken

A classic slow-cooked French dish in which the garlic suffuses the chicken with its rich flavour and provides a mellow purée to spread on the accompanying toast or baked potatoes.

serves 4

4 chicken legs, separated into
   drumsticks and thighs
salt and freshly ground black pepper
3–4 heads garlic
130ml olive oil
1 bouquet garni of thyme, parsley,
   rosemary, bay leaf and sage

Preheat the oven to 180°C/350°F/gas mark 4. Season the chicken and put it into an earthenware casserole. Separate the garlic cloves, discarding the outer skin, but don't peel the cloves. Add them to the casserole, trickle over the oil and turn everything with your hands to ensure that the garlic and chicken are well coated. Tuck the bouquet garni into the centre. Cover with foil and a well-fitting lid and bake low down in the oven for 1½ hours.

The chicken will be very tender, the garlic will squeeze easily from its skin and the aromas will be heady. Serve straight from the casserole, either with lightly toasted country bread on which to spread the garlic purée, or with potatoes that have been baked in the oven at the same time.

Chicken with green masala

Green masala, made with green chillies and coriander, and sometimes mint, is a popular flavouring in Goa. Here, it is used to marinate the chicken, which is then simmered in coconut milk.

serves 4

50g ginger, chopped
2 cloves garlic, chopped
4–5 green chillies, seeded and sliced
15g coriander leaves and
   young stems
salt
lemon juice or water
750g chicken breasts and/or
   thighs, skin removed and boned
1 tablespoon sunflower oil
about 200ml coconut milk

Put the ginger, garlic, chillies, coriander and salt to taste into a food processor and blend to a paste with a little lemon juice or water. Cut the chicken pieces in half, or in three if very large, put them into a bowl and coat them with the masala paste. Cover and leave to marinate for 30 minutes.

Heat the oil in a large, preferably nonstick, frying pan and fry the pieces of chicken, turning them once. Pour over the coconut milk, let it simmer for 10–15 minutes so that it thickens slightly to form a sauce for the chicken. Serve with rice.

Roast goose with prunes and apples

Goose is the only domesticated bird that is truly seasonal. A young goose, no more than 5kg, is best for roasting; older birds can be tough and are better braised. Goose gives off a lot of fat when cooking, so put it on a rack in a deep roasting tin. Be attentive to the cooking time; overcooked goose is stringy instead of moist. The prunes and apples, a traditional Danish accompaniment, are cooked separately.

serves 8–10

250g prunes

port or sweet sherry

1 goose weighing 4.5–5kg

salt and freshly ground black pepper

1–1.5kg parboiled potatoes,
    quartered

100g sugar

4–5 medium cooking apples, peeled,
    cored and cut in half horizontally

15g butter mashed with
    1 tablespoon plain flour

2–3 tablespoons redcurrant jelly
    (optional)

Cover the prunes in cold water and bring to the boil. Drain and pour over enough port or sherry to cover. Bring to the boil and simmer for 15 minutes until tender. Set aside and leave to cool in the liquor until needed.

An hour before you are ready to roast the goose, rub salt into the skin. Preheat the oven to 220°C/425°F/gas mark 7. Cover the breast with greaseproof paper or foil and put the bird on a rack in a large roasting tin. Roast for 30 minutes, then turn the oven down to 170°C/325°F/gas mark 3. Baste the bird with the fat in the tin, and remove the fat from the tin with a ladle or baster at regular intervals. Calculate the cooking time at 20 minutes per 500g; it will take 3 hours or a little longer in total. Halfway through, add the potatoes to the tin, making sure there is not too much fat. For the last half hour of cooking, remove the paper from the breast of the goose so that the skin will become golden and crisp.

Boil the sugar and 350ml of water for 5 minutes to make a syrup and poach the apples in it over a low heat, a few pieces at a time. They should be soft, but not overcooked. Lift the apple halves out with a slotted spoon. Drain and stone the prunes, reserving the liquor, fill the apple hollows with the prunes and keep warm.

The goose is cooked when the juices run clear if you insert the point of a knife in the thickest part of the thigh. Remove the potatoes from the tin and keep warm in the oven. Let the goose rest for 20 minutes in a warm place, loosely covered, to let the flesh relax before carving. Pour off all the fat from the roasting tin and add 150ml of the liquor from the prunes and 300ml of water, bring to the boil on the hob, stirring and scraping the bottom of the tin. Add small pieces of butter and flour, stirring each one in before adding more, until the gravy has thickened. If you wish, add redcurrant jelly. Serve the goose with the apples and prunes, the gravy, roast potatoes and Red Cabbage with Apple and Cranberries (see page 140).

Duck in hazelnut sauce

This Spanish dish can be made using a whole duck, cut into four pieces, or with the legs of two ducks, saving the breasts for grilling or roasting. The combination of nuts, garlic, parsley, wine or sherry, and sometimes tomato is a classic Spanish preparation that can be used with other poultry.

serves 4

4 duck legs, or I duck cut into
    4 pieces
I onion, chopped
4 cloves garlic, chopped
200g tomatoes, peeled and
    chopped, or use tinned
I teaspoon pimentón
    (see page II8)
salt, to taste
100g hazelnuts, roasted, skins
    removed and ground
    (see page 78)
150ml dry sherry
2 tablespoons chopped parsley

Remove any surplus fat from the duck pieces. Heat a large frying pan and put in the duck, skin-side down. Brown the pieces on all sides, remove them with a slotted spoon and set aside. Pour off all but I tablespoon of the fat from the pan (keep it for roasting potatoes). Fry the onion until golden, add the garlic and fry a moment longer, then stir in the tomatoes. Season with pimentón and salt, stir in the hazelnuts, sherry and parsley and simmer for a few minutes. Liquidise the sauce until it is fairly smooth.

Return the sauce to the pan, put back the pieces of duck, cover and simmer for about I hour, or until the duck is tender. Turn the pieces once or twice while the dish is cooking and add a little water if the sauce seems too thick. Saffron or Plain Mash (see page 160) or Glazed Sweet Potatoes (see page 154) go well with the duck, as do cabbage or spinach.

Note

If you use a whole duck, you can add the liver to the sauce. Clean and chop it into large pieces and fry it for 1–2 minutes before frying the onion. Add it to the liquidiser along with the other sauce ingredients.

Duck with vanilla

I ate this dish on the island of La Réunion in the Indian Ocean. It was here that the French planted vanilla at the beginning of the 19th century, but the plants were sterile, until a young slave, Edmond Albius, found a way to fertilise the flowers by hand. Since then, vanilla vines all over the world have been fertilised in the same way.

serves 4

4 duck breasts

1 onion, finely sliced

1 carrot, finely sliced

2 tomatoes, peeled and chopped

2 vanilla pods, split

1 teaspoon vanilla extract
or powder

Heat a nonstick dry pan and sear the breasts, skin-side down, for 5 minutes so that the fat runs out. Remove the duck, drain off all but 1 tablespoon of the fat, and cook the onion, carrot and tomato for 5 minutes. Return the duck breasts to the pan with the vanilla beans and extract and enough water to prevent sticking. Cover tightly and simmer for 40–45 minutes.

Transfer the duck pieces to a serving platter, crush the vegetables into the liquid to make a thicker sauce and pour this around the breasts. Garnish the dish with the split vanilla beans.

Guinea fowl with blackberry sauce

The people of Georgia use an abundance of fruit and nuts in savoury dishes. Pomegranates, grapes, plums, cherries, apricots and the ever-popular walnuts are used with all kinds of fish, meat and poultry. In Georgia, blackberry sauce is served with roast chicken, but it is a good match for the slightly gamey flavour of guinea fowl.

serves 2–3

for the sauce

450g blackberries

½ clove garlic, crushed with a
    little salt

½ teaspoon hot paprika

½ teaspoon ground ginger

2 teaspoons ground almonds

2 teaspoons lemon juice

3 tablespoons chopped coriander

1 guinea fowl

75g butter or 4 tablespoons olive oil

It is best to prepare the sauce an hour or so ahead so that the flavours have time to blend. Purée the blackberries and sieve to remove the seeds. Combine with the other sauce ingredients, taste and add more lemon juice if necessary. Cover and set aside.

Preheat the oven to 200°C/400°F/gas mark 6. Rub the guinea fowl with butter or olive oil and roast for 20 minutes per 500g. Check regularly that it is not becoming too dry or browned, and if necessary, cover with foil. Leave to stand for 10 minutes before carving and serving at once with the sauce.

Braised partridges with apple and figs

Their subtle, delicate flavour makes partridges my favourite game birds. If you are sure you have young partridges they are superb plain roasted; if you aren't, it is better to braise them. Most often paired with cabbage, partridges go well with fresh and dried fruit and nuts, and a dish of lentils makes a good accompaniment.

serves 2

2 tablespoons olive oil

2 partridges

2 medium onions, chopped

1 apple, peeled and quartered

4 dried figs, sliced

salt and freshly ground black pepper

pinch of nutmeg

200ml white wine

80ml double cream

1 teaspoon lemon juice

Heat the oil in an ovenproof casserole and brown the partridges. Remove them from the pan and fry the onion until soft. Put back the partridges, tuck the apple and figs around them, season with salt, pepper and nutmeg, and pour over the wine. Simmer for 10 minutes. Add enough water just to cover the birds, cover the casserole tightly and simmer for 1 hour. Check to see if the partridges are tender; if they are old they may need up to 30 minutes longer.

Transfer the birds to a serving dish and keep warm. Blend the cooking juices in a food processor or blender, stir in the cream and lemon juice, heat through and pour over the birds.

Partridges with white beans and chocolate sauce

In Mexico, the home of the cocoa bean, chocolate is used to spice and thicken moles – sauces for the indigenous turkey and other poultry. The inspiration for this dish comes from there, but this sauce is much less complex than a mole.

serves 2

200g haricot beans, soaked
  overnight, or use tinned
1 bouquet garni
salt and freshly ground black pepper
2 tablespoons olive oil
2 partridges, split in two and
  backbone removed
30g cubed pancetta or lardons
4 cloves garlic, chopped
strip of orange peel
1 bay leaf
125ml red wine
15g good-quality bitter chocolate

Drain the beans, put them into a pan with the bouquet garni and about 1 litre of water. Bring to the boil, skim the surface if necessary, then cover and simmer for 1 hour or more until the beans are just tender. Add salt 5 minutes before the end of the cooking time. Remove from the heat and keep warm in a little of the cooking water.

Heat the oil in a heavy pan and brown the partridges. Add the pancetta and toss in the oil. As it begins to colour, stir in the garlic, orange peel and bay leaf. Pour over the wine and enough water to come halfway up the birds. Season lightly, cover and simmer for about 30 minutes, turning the partridges once or twice.

When the partridges are tender, lift them out. Discard the orange peel and bay leaf. Taste the beans, and reheat gently if necessary. Grate the chocolate into the sauce, while stirring over a low heat. It will thicken quite quickly. Strain the beans and put them onto a serving platter, arrange the partridges on top, spoon over the sauce and serve.

Georgian pheasant

The improbable-sounding list of ingredients may deter you from trying this recipe, but do not be put off; the fruit and nuts form a well-flavoured sauce that complements the slightly dry flesh of the pheasant.

serves 2–3

50g hazelnuts

1 teaspoon green tea or 1 green
   tea bag

250g white grapes

juice of 1 orange

2 tablespoons port or Marsala

salt and freshly ground black pepper

1 pheasant

20g butter

Preheat the oven to 180°C/350°F/gas mark 4. Roast the hazelnuts in the oven for about 10 minutes until the skins become loose. Rub them in a tea towel to remove the skins and grind the nuts in a food processor. Pour 100ml of water over the tea and leave to infuse for 10 minutes, then strain. Liquidise the grapes and sieve to obtain the juice. Combine the hazelnuts, tea, grape juice, orange juice and port or Marsala.

Season the pheasant, rub with butter and place into an oval casserole that fits it snugly. Pour over the sauce, cover tightly and bake for 1 hour or until the pheasant is tender, basting occasionally. Carve and serve with the sauce.

Boeuf à la ficelle

Suspending a piece of meat in simmering stock and letting it poach is an old method of cooking. In the past, large joints were hung over huge cauldrons on open fires and left to simmer for hours. Using the method for a fillet of beef means that in 15 minutes, you have a perfectly cooked piece of meat, pink in the centre, with pure, concentrated flavours. If you have a larger piece of fillet, increase the poaching time slightly. Any meat leftover is excellent cold.

serves 4

2 litres very good beef stock

1 large bouquet garni of leek, bay
   leaf, thyme and parsley

1 piece of beef fillet, weighing
   about 1kg

Simmer the stock along with 1 litre of water and the bouquet garni for 20 minutes in a pan large enough to hold the meat. Trim the meat of any trace of silvery membrane and fat. If you have an end piece, fold under the tapering end. Tie the fillet at 4cm intervals, so that it will hold its shape while cooking. Thread a long string under the ties and tie the ends to a wooden spoon. With the stock at a steady simmer, lower the fillet into it, resting the spoon across the top of the pan. The meat should be suspended in the stock, not resting on the bottom of the pan. Bring back to a gentle simmer and cook for 12–15 minutes for very rare to rare meat; 20 minutes for medium rare.

Serve with Horseradish Mash (see page 160) and Baked Onions (see page 148).

Note
To reheat any leftovers, bring the stock to the boil, turn off the heat and put the meat in for 2 minutes. Lift out and slice.

Variation
The beef can also be cooked in a stock flavoured with oriental spices; replace the bouquet garni with a 100g spice bag (see page 96) and use 250ml of soy sauce instead of some of the water. Simmer together for 20 minutes before adding the beef.

Pot-roasted beef with mushrooms

A pot-roasted joint looks grander than a stew, although the cooking process is very similar. Pot-roasting uses less liquid, so remember to turn the meat and baste it from time to time. The flavours of the three mushrooms give this dish a pleasantly earthy flavour.

serves 4

2 tablespoons olive oil

1kg top rump, trimmed of excess fat

1 onion, finely sliced

½ teaspoon ground allspice

4 cloves

½ teaspoon freshly ground black pepper

5g dried ceps, soaked for 20 minutes in hot water to cover

handful of celery leaves, chopped, or 1 stalk celery, finely sliced

salt, to taste

100ml red wine

4 large field mushrooms, sliced

200g chestnut mushrooms, sliced

Take a heavy pan with a tight-fitting lid, preferably one that is not too much bigger than the piece of meat and heat 1 tablespoon of oil in it. Brown the meat on all sides and then remove it. Sauté the onion and spices in the pan for a few minutes. Drain the ceps, reserving the liquid. Chop them and add to the pan with the celery leaves and salt. Return the meat to the pan, pour over the wine and strained mushroom water and let the liquids bubble for a minute or so. Cover tightly; if necessary put a piece of foil under the lid. Lower the heat so that the liquid barely simmers, or transfer the pan to the oven preheated to 170°C/325°F/gas mark 3. Leave to simmer for 20 minutes, then add the field mushrooms. Continue to cook for a further 1–1½ hours, turning the meat once or twice.

Sauté the chestnut mushrooms in the remaining oil. Slice the beef and arrange on a warm serving platter. Spoon over the mushrooms and juices from the pan and top with the chestnut mushrooms.

Daube of beef

This slow-cooked Provençal stew has been a winter stand-by in our house for years. It is essentially Elizabeth David's recipe from *French Provincial Cooking*. I remember being drawn into it by its instruction to cut the beef into 'squares about the size of half a postcard' and the use of the strip of orange peel. This was clearly going to be something different from a hotpot or an English stew. And so it is. I always make it in a large quantity, whether for a dinner party or to have some leftover for another day, but you can, of course, reduce the amounts given by half.

serves 8–10

2kg top rump of beef

4 tablespoons olive oil

300g salt pork or streaky bacon in 1 piece, diced

4 onions, sliced

3 carrots, sliced

4 tomatoes, peeled and chopped

salt and freshly ground black pepper

4 cloves garlic, crushed

1 large bouquet garni of thyme, parsley, bay leaf and a strip of orange peel

250ml red wine

for the persillade

a few stalks of parsley, leaves picked and finely chopped

1 large clove garlic, finely chopped

1 tablespoon finely chopped capers

Preheat the oven to 150°C/300°F/gas mark 2. Trim the beef and cut it into squares about the size of half a postcard and almost 1cm thick. Pour the oil into a wide earthenware or cast-iron ovenproof casserole, add the salt pork and vegetables, and season. Arrange the meat over the top in overlapping layers. Bury the garlic and the bouquet garni in the centre. Season the upper layers. With the casserole open, start cooking on top of the stove. After about 10 minutes, pour the wine into a small pan, bring it to a fast boil and set light to it. Rotate the pan so that the flames spread. When they have died down, pour the wine, bubbling, over the meat. Cover the pot with greaseproof paper or foil and a well-fitting lid and transfer it to the oven. Leave for 3 hours. Check to see that the meat is tender.

While the daube is cooking, make a persillade by mixing together the parsley, garlic and capers. To serve, arrange the meat, salt pork and whole pieces of vegetable on a warm serving dish. Skim any excess fat from the sauce and pour this over and around the meat. Sprinkle the persillade over the top and serve with noodles or rice.

Carbonada criolla

This warming beef and vegetable stew, combining Old and New World ingredients, is a classic creole dish from Chile. That also means that there are many interpretations, as each household has its own version.

serves 6

800g lean beef, cubed
1 tablespoon paprika
2 tablespoons sunflower oil
1 onion, chopped
1 red pepper, seeds and ribs
    removed, cut into squares
1 green or red chilli, seeded and
    chopped
2 cloves garlic, chopped
1 large potato, peeled and cubed
1 sweet potato, peeled and cubed
2 carrots, chopped
salt and freshly ground black pepper
1 bouquet garni of thyme, parsley
    and oregano
about 1 litre beef stock
150g cooked white beans
kernels from 1 ear of corn, or
    100g tinned or frozen kernels

Sauté the beef and paprika in the oil in a large pan, turning the meat so that it browns evenly. Add the onion, red pepper, chilli and garlic and cook until the onion and pepper are soft. Add the 2 potatoes and carrots, season, and tuck in the bouquet garni. Pour over the stock. Bring to the boil, lower the heat, then cover and simmer for 45–50 minutes until the beef and vegetables are tender. Check while the carbonada is cooking and add a little more stock or water if needed. Add the beans and corn and simmer for a further 5 minutes. Serve alone or with rice, if you wish.

Stir-fried beef with Chinese greens

This winter dish from Sichuan is just as welcome here in winter, and it is quickly made. You could use sliced celery, broccolini or Chinese cabbage instead of the mustard greens.

serves 6

800g lean beef, such as sirloin
   or rump
80ml soy sauce
60ml rice or wine vinegar
3cm ginger, peeled and shredded
2 cloves garlic, finely sliced
2 red chillies, seeded and
   finely sliced
4 spring onions, finely sliced
2 teaspoons sugar
4 tablespoons sunflower oil
500g mustard greens, trimmed
   and shredded
peel from 1 well-scrubbed
   tangerine, cut into long strips
2 teaspoons sesame oil

Discard any fat on the beef and cut it into thin strips. Mix together the soy sauce, vinegar, ginger, garlic, chillies, spring onions and sugar and marinate the beef in it for 30 minutes.

Heat a wok or large frying pan and when it is very hot, pour in half the oil, swirling it around to coat the sides. Stir-fry the greens for 3 minutes and remove them from the wok. Drain the beef, reserving the marinade. Heat the remaining oil in the wok and when it is very hot, add the tangerine peel and the beef. Toss and stir rapidly for 1 minute. Return the greens to the wok, mix them well with the beef and pour over the marinade. Cook for 1 minute, then stir in the sesame oil. Remove from the heat, discard the strips of peel and serve with rice or noodles.

Hortobágy pancakes

This wonderfully filling dish originates from the Hortobágy Puszta, the vast plains of eastern Hungary. I used to eat it at the Gay Hussar restaurant in Soho, where it was one of my favourite dishes. Until I found myself travelling from Budapest to the eastern city of Debrecen – in order to inspect a new paperback printing press, with which the Hungarians hoped my employers, Penguin Books, would place orders – I was ignorant about its origins. As an editor, not a production manager, I had no idea about printing presses, as I tried to make clear to my hosts, but I did find out where the pancakes come from. The plains we crossed were unending, broken only by herds of cattle and flocks of sheep tended by herdsmen wrapped in great coats and hats (it was in March), and strange-looking wells with buckets suspended on long poles. The perspective is infinite and the silence profound. The food here is simple, and largely based on meat, either stewed or grilled.

On first reading, the recipe may seem daunting, but it is simplicity itself; the various parts integrating seamlessly into a sequence which may keep you occupied for about an hour and a half, but at a leisurely pace with plenty of time for the occasional sip of Bull's Blood.

serves 4

for the pancakes
200g flour (for best results use
    150g plain and 50g buckwheat)
2 eggs plus 1 egg yolk
pinch of salt
250ml milk, plus extra for thinning
150ml soda water

for the filling
600g lean veal, diced
2 medium onions, finely chopped
2–3 tablespoons lard, butter or oil
1 teaspoon salt
2 teaspoons paprika
2 tablespoons soured cream
500g spinach, large stalks removed
    (or 200g frozen chopped spinach)

for the sauce
20g plain flour, sieved
1 tablespoon paprika
200ml soured cream

First make the pancake batter, as it has to rest for an hour or so before use. Sift the flour into a large bowl, drop in the eggs and extra yolk, and add the salt. Stir the mixture with a whisk and gradually pour in the milk and soda water until the batter has the consistency of single cream. Set aside.

To make the filling, sauté the veal and onions in the lard with the salt and paprika for a few minutes, then cover the pan and cook gently for another 5 minutes. Drain off most of the juice, and reserve. Add the soured cream to the pan and simmer, on a heat diffuser, for about 30 minutes.

Meanwhile, cook the spinach leaves for 6–8 minutes in the water that still clings to them from washing. Drain into a colander and push out as much water as possible. Chop coarsely, add the spinach to the meat mixture and continue simmering for another 15–30 minutes; the meat should be very tender.

Put the oven on low. While the mixture is still simmering, make the pancakes. If the batter has thickened while standing, add enough milk to get it to a creamy consistency again. The mixture will make 8 sturdy pancakes (use about 75ml of batter for each) which will benefit from rather slow cooking. Stack them on a plate between sheets of kitchen paper. Keep warm in the oven.

To make the sauce, whisk the flour into the reserved pan juices and stir this and the paprika into the soured cream. Bring to a simmer and leave for a few minutes to lose the rawness of the paprika. There should be enough to cover the pancakes. If the sauce seems too thick, stir in a little water.

When the meat and spinach mixture is ready, divide it into 8 portions. Arrange each of these in a line across the middle of each pancake, leaving a little room at the sides. Fold the near end over, then roll the pancakes up, turning in the sides to make a parcel. Put them (outer fold down) on 2 ovenproof plates large enough to hold 4 each. Pour the sauce over the pancakes and return to the oven for 5–10 minutes to heat through. Serve the first plateful while keeping the second serving warm in the oven.

Liver with hazelnut and garlic sauce

Calf's liver is prized for its delicate flavour and smooth texture. Lamb's liver is slightly darker in colour and very tender. Both respond well to rapid grilling or sautéing, as in this Spanish dish with its rich hazelnut and garlic sauce.

serves 4

4 cloves garlic, peeled

2 tablespoons olive oil

1 slice bread, crust removed,
    soaked in 2–3 tablespoons
    wine vinegar

8 hazelnuts, roasted and skins
    removed (see page 78)

2 tablespoons chopped parsley

stock or water

500g lamb's or calf's liver, cleaned
    and cut into strips

salt and freshly ground black pepper

Fry the garlic cloves in the olive oil until golden. Transfer them to a mortar or food processor and crush or blend to a thick paste with the bread, nuts and parsley. Dilute the mixture with a little stock or water to make a thick sauce.

Heat the oil again and sauté the liver until lightly coloured. Season with salt and pepper. Add the mixture from the mortar. Let it come to a bare simmer, giving 1 or 2 bubbles and serve at once. Be careful not to overcook the liver or it will be tough. The whole process should take no more than 10 minutes.

Liver with paprika

This dish of Czech origin makes a quick supper with rice or mashed potatoes and a salad. As an alterantive to finishing it with soured cream, use 150g chopped tomatoes and a few chopped rosemary leaves to make the sauce.

serves 4

500g calf's liver, cleaned and cut
    into thin strips

plain flour seasoned with salt,
    freshly ground black pepper
    and 1 tablespoon paprika

60g butter

2 cloves garlic, crushed

1 small glass white wine

handful of chopped parsley

150ml soured cream

Coat the liver in the seasoned flour. Melt the butter in a heavy pan and add the liver and garlic. Sauté for 2–3 minutes over a high heat, turning the liver until it is evenly browned.

Scoop out the liver and keep warm while finishing the sauce. Add the wine to the pan, scrape loose any bits sticking to the bottom and squash the garlic to incorporate it into the sauce. Bring to the boil, reduce the heat and stir in the parsley and the cream. Return the liver to the pan, let it heat through and serve.

Oxtail with sauerkraut

Long, slow braising transforms tough oxtail into tender, well-flavoured chunks of meat. The sauerkraut adds a typical central European note and makes a mellow-tasting dish after slow-cooking with the oxtail. The dish can be reheated gently if made in advance.

serves 4

3 tablespoons sunflower oil

1kg oxtail pieces

100g smoked back bacon, cut into large pieces

15g dried ceps, soaked in hot water to cover

3 large carrots, cut into chunks

2 large onions, cut into chunks

2 bay leaves

a few sprigs of thyme

3 cloves garlic, chopped

150ml red wine

freshly ground black pepper

1 large jar or tin of sauerkraut, 800g–1kg

Preheat the oven to 150°C/300°F/gas mark 2. Heat the oil in a heavy ovenproof casserole, trim any excess fat from the oxtail pieces and brown on all sides in. Add half of the bacon pieces and let them colour. Strain the ceps, reserving the liquid, but discard any grit or dirt. Add the ceps to the pan with the carrots, onions, herbs and garlic. Pour over the wine, the cep liquid, and a little water. Season with pepper. Bring to the boil, cover tightly with foil and a lid, and transfer to the oven. Braise for about 2 hours until the meat starts to become tender.

Rinse the sauerkraut in cold water to rid it of excess salt. If it still seems too salty, soak for 15 minutes in cold water and drain. Remove the casserole from the oven, spread the sauerkraut over the oxtail and lay the remaining pieces of bacon on top. Cover tightly again and return the pan to the oven for another hour. Serve with boiled potatoes.

Lancashire hotpot

One of England's best winter dishes. It is always cheering to take a hotpot, with its nicely browned, bubbling potatoes, out of the oven. Originally made in tall earthenware pots in which chops could stand upright, the dish is now layered in round-bellied pots, but any deep earthenware casserole can be used.

serves 8

8 middle neck lamb chops, trimmed of excess fat

1kg potatoes, peeled and sliced 5mm thick

Preheat the oven to 170°C/325°F/gas mark 3. Fry the lamb chops in a frying pan in their own fat until browned on both sides. Put a layer of potatoes in the bottom of the casserole pot along with the bay leaf. Put some of the chops on top, followed by a layer of onions and kidneys. Season each layer with salt and pepper. Continue making layers, finishing with a

1 bay leaf
500g onions, thinly sliced
4 lamb's kidneys, cleaned and sliced
salt and freshly ground black pepper
300ml stock
lard or butter

layer of potatoes, overlapping them 'like slates on a roof'. Pour over the stock, dot the top with lard or butter, cover tightly (if necessary put a piece of foil or greaseproof paper under the lid) and transfer to the oven to cook very slowly for about 2½ hours. Remove the lid (and foil, if used) and cook for another 20 minutes to brown the potatoes; turn up the heat if necessary. Serve straight from the pot.

Variations
Add a few sliced carrots or sliced mushrooms to the layers in the pot.
Add 1 or 2 small black puddings, as was traditionally done in Cumbria.

Slow-roast leg of lamb

One of my favourite ways of cooking lamb, and utterly foolproof – it makes a splendid appearance at the table, too. Just about any vegetables or pulses can accompany it, from aubergines to okra or a potato gratin.

serves 6
3 cloves garlic
2 tablespoons mixed dried herbs
    (such as thyme, oregano, savory,
    rosemary)
salt and freshly ground black pepper
2kg leg of lamb, trimmed of
    excess fat
3 tablespoons olive oil
1 large glass white wine or Marsala
1 salt-preserved lemon

Preheat the oven to 150°C/300°F/gas mark 2. Crush the garlic to a paste with the herbs and a little salt. Make slits around the leg and push a little paste into each. Rub the lamb with 1 tablespoon of oil, put the remaining oil into a heavy ovenproof casserole which fits the lamb snugly, and brown the lamb on all sides. Pour half the wine over the lamb, cover the casserole with the lid or a double layer of foil, and roast in the oven for 3½–4 hours, turning the meat once every hour. It should be very tender but not completely falling off the bone.

While it is cooking, chop the peel of the lemon into small pieces and discard the flesh. Lift the meat from the roasting tin, cover with foil and keep warm. Pour off excess fat from the tin, blot more with kitchen paper if necessary, and add the remaining wine to deglaze the pan. Stir in the lemon peel and season with black pepper; the lemon should provide enough salt. Serve this sauce with the lamb, which will carve easily into thick slices.

Roast rack of lamb with dukka

Dukka is an Egyptian nut and spice blend that varies from family to family. It can be sprinkled over rice or soup, and on pieces of warm pita dunked in olive oil it is one of the best nibbles to serve with drinks. It also makes an excellent crust for lamb. Some spice merchants now sell ready-made dukka, but I have given a recipe below because it is easy to make at home, and keeps well.

serves 2

for the dukka
100g hazelnuts
75g sesame seeds
60g coriander seeds
30g cumin seeds
salt, to taste

1 rack of lamb
olive oil

To make the dukka, dry roast all the nuts and seeds separately until the hazelnuts lose their skins, the sesame seeds are golden, and the coriander and cumin darken and give off their aroma. Remove the loose skins from the hazelnuts (see page 78). Put the hazelnuts, sesame seeds, coriander and cumin into a food processor with a little salt and grind to a coarse powder. Don't overwork it or the oil from the nuts and sesame will be released and turn it into a paste. It can now be stored in an airtight container.

Preheat the oven to 220°C/425°F/gas mark 7. Rub the lamb with olive oil and press 2–3 tablespoons of dukka into the fat side. Roast for 20 minutes if you like your lamb rare, or a few minutes longer for medium rare.

Serve with Provençal Lentils (see page 150) and Roast Fennel and Onions (see page 145).

Spiced lamb shanks

Lamb shanks offer great value for money, are quick to prepare and can be left to simmer for a couple of hours to produce a rich, succulent dish.

serves 4

4 lamb shanks, trimmed of
  excess fat

2 tablespoons olive oil

¾ teaspoon ground cinnamon

¾ teaspoon ground ginger

Brown the lamb shanks in the oil in a large pan. Remove them and set aside while you fry the spices lightly in the oil. Add the onion and fry with the spices for 4–5 minutes, then put back the lamb shanks. Add the tomatoes, salt and enough stock or water almost to cover the shanks. Bring to the boil, cover and simmer on a heat diffuser or in the oven preheated to 150°C/300°F/gas mark 2. It will take 2–2½ hours.

½ teaspoon ground cumin

½ teaspoon ground allspice

¼ teaspoon grated nutmeg

1 large onion, chopped

400g chopped tinned tomatoes

1 teaspoon salt

about 250ml chicken stock or water

Lift the shanks out of the pan carefully; the meat will be loose on the bone. Put them in a covered bowl while you boil the cooking liquid on the stove to reduce it slightly and then blend it to make a sauce. Strain it into the rinsed-out pan, put back the lamb and reheat gently if necessary.

Serve with Soft Polenta (see page 161), potatoes or couscous and a bowl of harissa.

Lamb steaks with pomegranate sauce

This dish has Middle Eastern origins. Fruit is often used to accompany meat, particularly lamb. Pomegranate molasses is sold in Middle Eastern shops and in some supermarkets. If you can't find it, use pomegranate juice and a little sugar.

serves 2

2 tablespoons sunflower oil

1 cardamom pod, crushed

3–4cm piece cinnamon, lightly
   crushed

1 clove

2 small pieces mace, lightly
   crushed

2 lamb leg steaks, about 200g
   each, boned

1 onion, sliced

2 cloves garlic, sliced

2 tablespoons pomegranate
   molasses

salt, to taste

1 tablespoon pomegranate seeds

mint leaves, to garnish

Heat the oil in a heavy pan and fry the spices. In the same pan, brown the meat on both sides, then add the onion and garlic. Let these colour lightly, then add the pomegranate molasses, season with salt to taste and pour over 60ml of water. Cover tightly and simmer for 45 minutes to 1 hour, depending on the thickness of the steaks. Turn them once while they are cooking.

Lift out the steaks and keep warm while you reduce the cooking liquid a little if necessary. Strain it over the meat and garnish with pomegranate seeds and a few mint leaves. The lamb goes well with rice, boiled potatoes or Swiss Chard and Potato (see page 138).

Braised pork belly with Chinese flavours

This is a dish to make in a large quantity for hungry friends on a chilly winter evening. Pork belly braises to a wonderfully melting texture, and soy sauce, garlic, ginger and other spices give a subtle background flavour. Chinese shops sell bags of 'assorted spices', usually weighing about 250g, which contain star anise, cassia or cinnamon, chilli, clove, dried ginger, fennel, dried tangerine peel and liquorice. In Chinese cooking, the spices are used to flavour a sauce for boiled meat. I use them to flavour the braising liquid. If you can't get to a Chinese shop, you should be able to assemble several of these whole spices from a supermarket and you can dry your own tangerine peel by removing all the pith and leaving it on a rack in a warm place for 4–5 days.

serves 6

1.7kg belly of pork, cut into
    6 thick slices
400ml soy sauce
300ml dry sherry or sake
100g whole dried spices (see
    above), tied in a piece of muslin
10 cloves garlic, peeled
8cm fresh ginger, sliced
80g sugar
1kg bok choi or other Chinese
    greens, trimmed
4 spring onions, thinly sliced

Bring the pork to the boil in a large pan of cold water and simmer for 10 minutes, discarding any scum. Drain the meat, rinse the pan and put back the meat together with 2 litres of water, the soy sauce, sherry or sake, spices, garlic, ginger and sugar. If necessary add a little more water; all the meat should be covered. If it keeps bobbing up, put a double piece of greaseproof paper or a small plate over the top of the liquid. Bring slowly to the boil and simmer gently for 2–2½ hours. The pork is ready when a skewer can be inserted easily.

Remove the pan from the heat, ladle about a quarter of the cooking stock into another pan and boil down steadily, until reduced by half. Check regularly that it does not become too salty because of the soy. While it is reducing, leave the pork in the remaining stock to keep warm.

Bring a large pan of water to the boil and blanch the bok choi for 2 minutes. Drain it carefully to remove all excess water and arrange in the centre of a large dish. Lift the pork out of the pan and place around the bok choi (the stock can be frozen and reused as a base for a similar Chinese dish). Spoon over some of the reduced sauce, scatter over the spring onions and serve.

Cuban roast pork

Versions of this dish are found in all the Spanish Caribbean islands and in South America. Sour orange juice is popular as a marinade for meat and fish, and flavourings vary from country to country – thyme, sage and nutmeg might replace oregano and allspice, but cumin is fairly constant.

serves 6–8

for the marinade

6 tablespoons Seville orange juice,
   or ½ sweet orange juice and
   ½ lime or lemon juice
1 tablespoon grated sweet
   orange rind
1 teaspoon ground cumin
1 teaspoon ground allspice
1½ teaspoons crushed dried
   oregano
½ teaspoon coarsely ground
   black pepper
4 cloves garlic, crushed
4 tablespoons sunflower oil

1.5kg loin of pork, boned, skin
   removed, rolled and tied
2 tablespoons sunflower oil
juice of ½ sweet orange
4 tablespoons port or sweet sherry

Blend all the marinade ingredients together. Put the pork into a dish, pour over the marinade and leave for at least 3–4 hours or up to 24 in the refrigerator. Turn occasionally, rubbing the marinade into the meat.

Preheat the oven to 200°C/400°F/gas mark 6. Wipe the meat and reserve the marinade. Heat the oil in a small roasting tin, add the pork and brown it quickly on all sides. Transfer the tin to the oven and roast for 30 minutes. Lift out the tin and reduce the heat to 170°C/325°F/gas mark 3. Baste the pork and pour off the fat. Pour the marinade over the pork and return the tin to the oven. Roast for a further hour, basting regularly so that the pork acquires a good glaze. Test that the meat juices run clear by piercing the pork through the centre with a fine skewer. Lift the pork from the tin and keep warm, covered with foil.

Transfer the roasting tin to the stove top, and scrape loose any bits stuck to the bottom. Add the sweet orange juice and the port or sherry and boil to deglaze the pan. If necessary add 1–2 tablespoons of water. Strain the juices and serve with the pork. Boiled potatoes and Okra with Apricots (see page 143) make good accompaniments.

Note
Seville oranges usually appear in the shops in January. The season is short so buy a quantity and store them, whole, in the freezer. Thaw as needed to provide juice for marinades later in the year.

Pork chops baked with sweet potatoes

A meal-in-a-dish supper that is adaptable to many flavours. Try sage, winter savory or rosemary instead of thyme, or use spices such as fennel seed, crushed coriander or juniper. Instead of the maple syrup or honey and cider combination use white wine or Marsala.

serves 2

3 tablespoons sunflower oil

250g sweet potatoes, sliced

salt and freshly ground black pepper

2 medium onions, sliced

3–4 sprigs thyme, leaves picked

2 pork loin chops, trimmed

1 tablespoon maple syrup or honey

75ml cider

Preheat the oven to 180°C/350°F/gas mark 4. Lightly oil a small gratin or similar ovenproof dish. Spread the sweet potato slices over the bottom of the dish and season with salt and pepper. Heat the rest of the oil in a frying pan and fry the onions until browned. Lift them out and spread them over the potatoes together with the leaves from a couple of sprigs of thyme. Add the chops to the frying pan, let them colour on both sides, season and put them on top of the vegetables. Scatter over the rest of the thyme leaves. Drizzle over the maple syrup or honey and add the cider. Cover the dish with foil and bake for 40 minutes. Remove the foil, lower the heat to 150°C/300°F/gas mark 2 and cook for a further 10 minutes to let the chops and potatoes brown slightly.

Gammon braised in cider

In the past, salted cuts of pork were often served with pease pudding, a sensible combination since both pulses and meat could be stored through the winter months. A bean or pea purée still makes a good accompaniment, or try the suggestions below.

serves 4

750g piece gammon, boned

1 sprig sage

4 sprigs thyme

1 stick celery, including leaves, sliced

1 carrot, sliced

1 onion, quartered

10 peppercorns

500ml cider

Put the gammon into a deep pan, cover with water, bring slowly to the boil and drain. Rinse under the cold tap and remove the skin and excess fat. Rinse out the pan and put back the gammon with the herbs, vegetables, peppercorns and cider along with sufficient water just to cover the meat. Bring to a simmer, and cook gently, covered, for about 1¼ hours, or until the gammon can be pierced easily with a skewer. Turn off the heat, and if necessary keep the gammon warm in the cooking water.

Slice the meat and serve with Dijon mustard and a Gratin of Winter Vegetables (see page 148) or with creamed spinach.

Bean, pumpkin and sausage casserole

Simple and sustaining, this is a comforting dish for dark winter evenings. Very long cooking may cause the pumpkin to collapse, but the flavour will still be good. Don't leave out the sage leaves; they add depth to the casserole.

serves 4

250g cannellini or haricot beans,
  soaked overnight and drained
salt and freshly ground black pepper
2 tablespoons olive or sunflower oil
8 small chorizo, Toulouse or
  similar sausages
1 large onion, sliced
150g bacon or salt pork, diced
4 cloves garlic, chopped
1½ teaspoons pimentón
  (see page 118)
½ teaspoon ground mace
½ teaspoon ground allspice
750g pumpkin or butternut
  squash, cubed
10 sage leaves
400g chopped tomatoes, fresh
  or tinned
3–4 tablespoons chopped parsley

Put the beans into a large pan, cover with 3 times their volume of water and bring to the boil. Boil for 10 minutes, then lower the heat and simmer until the beans are just soft, about 45 minutes to 1 hour, depending on their age. Season with a little salt in the last 5 minutes of cooking time. Drain the beans and set aside.

Heat the oil in a large heavy pan and fry the sausages, turning and stirring, for 10 minutes to brown them lightly. Lift out the sausages, put in the onion and bacon or salt pork and fry until the onion starts to colour. Stir in the garlic and spices, add the pumpkin and fry for 5 minutes, so that it colours on all sides. Add the sage leaves, tomatoes and beans and mix all the ingredients together gently. Season with salt and pepper, put back the sausages, burying them in the beans. Pour over enough boiling water just to cover. Cover with a lid and simmer over a low heat or put into the oven preheated to 150°C/300°F/gas mark 2 for 1–1½ hours, or longer. It is important to give time for the flavours to blend. If the casserole becomes too dry, top it up with a little more water. Stir in the parsley and serve.

Tourtière

This pie, made with pork or a mixture of pork and veal, is prepared throughout Quebec for the festive Christmas Eve dinner. It is very similar to the Alsatian Tourte de la Vallée de Munster, except that the Alsatians use bread soaked in milk, not potato. Perhaps Alsatian emigrants took the tourte to Quebec.

serves 6

1 medium potato, peeled and boiled

4 tablespoons milk

2 tablespoons sunflower oil

250g minced pork

250g minced veal

1 onion, chopped

½ teaspoon nutmeg

¼ teaspoon ground cloves

salt and freshly ground black pepper

a few sage leaves, shredded

600g ready-made puff pastry

1 egg, separated

Preheat the oven to 200°C/400°F/gas mark 6. Mash the potato and soak it in the milk. Heat the oil in a frying pan and fry the meat and onion, breaking up the meat with a wooden spoon. Season with the nutmeg, cloves, salt, pepper and sage. Cook until the meat juices have evaporated, about 12–15 minutes. Stir in the potato, mixing it well with the meat.

Divide the pastry in 2. Roll out 1 piece to a circle larger than a 26cm pie dish. Fit the pastry into the dish, spread the filling over it and brush the border with egg white. Roll out the second piece of pastry, cover the pie with it and crimp the edges. Make a hole in the centre, use a knife or fork to decorate the pastry if you wish, and paint it with egg yolk. Bake for 30–35 minutes until golden brown. Butternut and Green Bean Salad (see page 28), Moroccan Carrot Salad (see page 25) or Avocado, Pomegranate and Wild Rocket Salad (see page 27) make good accompaniments.

Seared venison medallions with sage butter

This dish takes minutes to prepare, looks stylish and tastes delicious. Small sprigs of rosemary could be used instead of sage leaves.

serves 4

600g venison fillet, cut into
  8 medallions

1 tablespoon chopped thyme

salt and freshly ground black pepper

16 thin rashers streaky bacon

50g butter

8 sage leaves

Sprinkle the medallions with the thyme and season with pepper and a little salt, if you wish (the bacon will be salty). Wrap each medallion in 2 rashers of bacon. Heat the butter in a heavy pan, add the sage leaves and the venison and fry slowly, turning the medallions once, until the bacon is crisp. Use 2 pans or fry in batches and keep warm if necessary. Serve the venison with the pan juices and sage leaves spooned over.

Gratin Savoyard (see page 159) goes well with this dish, as does savoy cabbage.

Variations

Omit the sage. When the medallions are cooked remove them from the pan and keep warm.

Deglaze the pan with 3 tablespoons of whisky. Add 120ml of beef stock and boil to reduce by half. Whisk in 50g of butter, cut in small pieces. Stir in 2 tablespoons of rinsed capers and 1 tablespoon of chopped parsley. Spoon the sauce onto plates and put the venison medallions on top.

Alternatively, deglaze the pan with 3 tablespoons of red wine. Add 120ml of beef stock and reduce by half. Add a squeeze of lemon juice or 1 tablespoon of redcurrant jelly, and stir in 80ml of soured cream. Spoon the sauce onto plates and put the medallions on top.

Venison chilli

Chilli may not be a sophisticated dish, but it is certainly popular and flavourful. Venison responds well to the rich spicy sauce, although chilli is traditionally made with pork or beef. This is not a very hot chilli; I prefer to use chillies such as anchos or guajillos which add flavour as much as heat. These Mexican dried chillies are now being sold in some supermarkets or are available from Mexican suppliers and spice merchants. If you can't get them, use 1½–2 tablespoons of good-quality ground chilli instead.

serves 6

4 ancho or guajillo chillies, stalks and seeds removed
3 tablespoons sunflower oil
2 onions, chopped
750g venison, diced (use shoulder, breast or meat sold as stewing venison)
4 cloves garlic, chopped
1½ teaspoons ground cumin
1½ teaspoons dried oregano
salt and freshly ground black pepper
1 tablespoon tomato purée
400g tinned chopped tomatoes
500ml beef stock
2 tablespoons red wine vinegar
800g tinned red kidney beans

Heat a heavy dry frying pan or griddle and toast the chillies over a moderate heat, turning them with tongs, until they have softened. It will take 10–15 minutes. Transfer them to a bowl and cover with boiling water. Put a small plate on top to keep the chillies submerged and soak for 30 minutes. Remove them from the water and put them into a blender with about 250ml of the soaking liquid and purée them.

Heat the oil in a large casserole and fry the onions . When they start to brown, add the venison and brown on all sides. Add the garlic, cumin, oregano, salt and pepper, the chilli purée, tomato purée and tomatoes. Stir well and pour over the stock. Cover the pan tightly and simmer over a very low heat for 2 hours, or put the casserole into a preheated oven at 170°C/325°F/gas mark 3.

Check the venison is done, then stir in the vinegar and beans. Simmer, uncovered, for 10 minutes. Serve at once, or leave overnight and reheat slowly; the flavours will improve.

Braised hare

Hare is at its best during the autumn and winter months, when it is often available at farmers' markets as well as from game suppliers and some butchers. It can sometimes be bought jointed and pre-packed, but a butcher will joint a whole animal for you. The meat is lean, savoury and dark in colour. Several hours in a marinade will enhance its flavour and tenderness.

serves 6–8

500ml red wine

6 tablespoons olive oil

8 juniper berries, crushed

8 allspice berries, crushed

8 black peppercorns, crushed

3 bay leaves

1 tablespoon thyme leaves

1 hare, jointed

8–10 cloves garlic, peeled

salt, to taste

80ml port

1–2 tablespoons redcurrant jelly

45g butter

1 tablespoon plain flour

2–3 bunches spring onions, trimmed to the same length

Put the wine, olive oil, juniper, allspice, peppercorns, bay leaves and thyme into a large bowl. Mix together and put in the pieces of hare. Cover the bowl and leave to marinate in the refrigerator for up to 24 hours, turning the pieces occasionally.

Preheat the oven to 170°C/325°F/gas mark 3. Turn the meat and marinade into a large earthenware casserole. Add the garlic cloves, season with salt and pour in 50ml of the port. Cover tightly (place a piece of foil under the lid if necessary) and simmer in the oven for about 2½ hours, or until the flesh is loose on the bones.

Lift out the pieces of hare and keep them warm. Pour the cooking juices into a pan and heat to reduce by about one third. Add the remaining port and the redcurrant jelly. Taste and adjust the seasoning if necessary, and simmer for a further 5 minutes. Remove the bay leaves, strain the juices into a bowl, pressing to push the garlic into the sauce. Pour the sauce back into the rinsed-out pan and put back on the heat. Mash together 15g of the butter and the flour and stir it, a piece at a time, into the sauce if the sauce is still thin. Wait after each addition so that you don't end up with a gluey texture.

While the sauce is simmering, heat the remaining butter in a wide frying pan and lightly brown the onions. Use them to garnish the hare and serve the sauce separately. Soft Polenta (see page 161) is a good accompaniment.

Rabbit with prunes and almonds

Farmers' markets sell wild rabbits, which goes some way to make up for their absence from many city butchers and supermarkets. The best rabbits are those that are imported from France – they are large, well-flavoured and succulent, and if you can carry back a rabbit or two from a French supermarket (where they are beautifully jointed and packed), do so. If you have wild rabbit, you will need two to feed four people.

serves 4

3 tablespoons olive oil

1 large rabbit, jointed

50g pancetta, cubed

6 shallots, finely chopped

salt and freshly ground black pepper

1 teaspoon finely chopped
   rosemary leaves

200ml sweet sherry or port

50g flaked almonds

12 ready-to-eat stoned prunes

Heat 2 tablespoons of the oil in a large, heavy pan and brown the rabbit pieces on all sides. Lift them out as they are ready and add the pancetta and shallots. Let them colour in the oil, then return the rabbit, season with salt and pepper and add the rosemary. Pour 150ml of sherry or port over the rabbit, let it bubble for a minute or so, then add 100ml of water. Cover the pan tightly, putting a layer of foil under the lid, if necessary. Braise the rabbit over a gentle heat for about 1½ hours, turning the pieces from time to time. They will take on a deep golden colour from the sherry. Check that the rabbit is tender by piercing the thickest part of the leg with a thin skewer.

About 20 minutes before the rabbit is ready, heat the remaining oil in a heavy pan and fry the almonds until lightly coloured. Add the prunes and the remaining sherry or port and simmer very gently for 5 minutes. Add this mixture to the rabbit for the last 10 minutes of cooking time.

Serve with Squash Purée (see page 155) or Glazed Sweet Potatoes (see page 154).

Rabbit braised with chestnuts and mushrooms

If you use a large rabbit, one will be enough, but you will need two small wild ones. Have the rabbit jointed into six pieces – legs, forelegs and ribs and the back cut in half. Wild mushrooms, such as ceps and chanterelles, or cultivated mushrooms, such as portobellos and crimini, will give the dish more flavour than standard cup mushrooms.

serves 4

4 tablespoons sunflower oil

50g butter

1 large rabbit, jointed

1 onion, finely sliced

salt and freshly ground black pepper

1 bouquet garni of thyme, rosemary, bay leaf and a small piece of cinnamon

150ml white wine

100ml stock or water

200g cooked chestnuts (see below)

200g mushrooms

200ml crème fraîche

Heat 2 tablespoons of the oil and half the butter in a large heavy pan and fry the pieces of rabbit until golden. Remove them to a plate and fry the onion until lightly coloured. Return the rabbit to the pan, season and tuck in the bouquet garni. Pour over the wine, let it reduce slightly, then add the stock or water. Cover the pan and let it simmer over a low heat for about 1 1/2 hours, or until the rabbit is tender when pierced with a skewer. Halfway through the cooking time, add the chestnuts and add a little more liquid if necessary. When the rabbit has 10 minutes of cooking time left, heat the remaining oil and butter in another pan, brush the mushrooms and sauté them.

Lift out the rabbit and chestnuts, place on a serving dish and keep warm. Discard the bouquet. There should be about a wine glass of liquid in the pan; if there is more, boil to reduce it. Stir in the crème fraîche, scraping up any bits from the bottom of the pan. Add the mushrooms, pour this sauce over the rabbit and serve. It makes a good dish on its own, but if you are very hungry serve it with buttered noodles.

Note

To peel chestnuts, cut across on the flat side, bring them to the boil in a pan of water, simmer for 5 minutes, then remove from the heat. Take out the chestnuts one at a time, and peel off the outer and inner skin. They only peel properly if they are hot, so if necessary put on gloves, and reheat the water if it gets too cool. Once peeled, boil or braise the chestnuts for 20–30 minutes.

Vacuum-packed chestnuts save greatly on the task of preparing fresh ones, so unless you have access to a harvest of chestnuts I suggest buying ready prepared ones. They can be used straight from the packet. Dried chestnuts must be soaked in water for several hours before cooking.

Russian cabbage and mushroom pie

Russians have a great love of pies, large and small, filled with meat, fish or vegetables. My cabbage and mushroom filling is not strictly authentic; Russians tend to use the vegetables separately as fillings, but I prefer this combination. Dill, fresh or dried, is a good alternative to sage to flavour the cabbage, and if you prefer nutmeg to mace, use a smaller amount. The pie can be made with puff pastry or shortcrust. It makes an impressive main course for a vegetarian meal.

serves 4–5

750g white cabbage, shredded

15g dried ceps, soaked for 20 minutes in hot water to cover

50g butter

2 onions, chopped

2 tablespoons chopped sage leaves

salt and freshly ground black pepper

300g field or portobello mushrooms, thickly sliced

¼ teaspoon mace or a grating of nutmeg

4 tablespoons soured cream

1 egg, beaten with a little milk or water

for the shortcrust pastry

340g plain flour, plus extra for dusting

¼ teaspoon salt

160g butter, cut into small pieces

1 egg yolk, lightly beaten (optional)

6–8 tablespoons iced water (more if needed)

for the optional sauce

100ml soured cream

liquor from soaking ceps reduced to 3 tablespoons

2 tablespoons chopped parsley

2 teaspoons dried dill

Make the pastry following the method on page 184. Blanch the cabbage for 5 minutes in boiling water and drain well. Drain the ceps, reserving the liquid, chop them and set aside. Melt the butter in a large pan and cook the onions gently until soft and lightly coloured. Add the cabbage, cover the pan and simmer for 20–30 minutes until the cabbage is tender. Remove the lid, raise the heat and cook briskly until the liquid in the pan has evaporated. Stir in the sage, season with salt and pepper and remove the pan from the heat.

Heat the mushrooms slowly in a large dry pan until they give off their juices. Turn up the heat, season with the mace or nutmeg, salt and pepper, then stir in the soured cream and the reconstituted ceps. Remove from the heat.

Preheat the oven to 200°C/400°F/gas mark 6. Roll out the pastry into 2 oblongs, one slightly larger than the other. Put the smaller one onto a baking sheet lined with foil (this helps remove the pie when it is baked). Put a layer of cabbage onto the pastry, leaving a 2cm border of pastry around the edge. Spread the mushrooms over the cabbage and top with the remaining cabbage. Brush the pastry edge with egg wash and cover with the second piece of pastry. Press the edges firmly together to seal. Cut a hole in the centre of the pie and brush all over with egg wash. Bake for 50–60 minutes until golden brown.

If you wish to serve the pie with the soured cream sauce, make it just before you remove the pie from the oven. Heat the cream gently and stir in the remaining ingredients.

Winter vegetable tart

This colourful tart makes a good main course for a vegetarian meal. The choice and quantities of the different vegetables can be varied to suit your taste, but keep the leek purée and the tomatoes, because their colour and shape look attractive among the other vegetables.

serves 6

60g butter, plus extra melted
   butter for the pastry (optional)
1kg leeks, thinly sliced
salt and freshly ground black pepper
2 red onions, cut into chunks
1 red and 1 yellow pepper, seeds and
   ribs removed, sliced
olive oil
750g butternut squash, peeled and
   cut into small chunks
150g small Brussels sprouts,
   trimmed
150g cooked chestnuts, broken in
   half (see page 108)
1 packet filo pastry
8–10 cherry tomatoes

Preheat the oven to 200°C/400°F/gas mark 6. Melt the butter in a wide heavy pan and gently sauté the leeks until very soft and almost reduced to a purée. Season and set them aside. Spread the onions and peppers on a baking tray, drizzle oil over them and put them into the oven to roast for about 20 minutes, turning them once. After 5 minutes, put the butternut pieces on another tray, drizzle with oil and put the tray in the oven. The vegetables on both trays should be softened and somewhat more than half cooked at the same time. Meanwhile, cook the sprouts in boiling water for 5–6 minutes, then drain them. Remove the roasted vegetables from the oven, reduce the oven temperature to 180°C/350°F/gas mark 4, and mix them together with the sprouts and the chestnuts. Season well and set aside.

Put a 28cm loose-bottomed flan tin on a baking sheet and surround it with a collar of crumpled foil to support the overhanging pastry. Brush the tin with oil. Keep the filo pastry under a damp tea towel and work with 2 sheets at a time. Brush them with olive oil or melted butter and spread them over the base of the tart. Brush 2 more sheets and place them in the tin at different angles so that they overlap, covering part of the bottom, and their upper corners hang over the edge of the tin. Continue with other sheets of pastry in the same way so that the upper corners hang over the edge at intervals all around the tin. Sheets of filo vary in size, so it is difficult to give an exact number to line the tin, 10–14 should be enough. Brush the upper corners of the pastry with a little more oil or butter.

Spread the leeks over the base of the tart, then cover them with the vegetable mixture. Pierce the base of each tomato with the point of a small sharp knife and add these to the tart. Bake the tart for 20–25 minutes until the pastry is crisp and the vegetables on top are lightly golden. Carefully remove the foil collar and the outer rim of the tin, and put the tart on a serving dish. This tart does quite well on its own, but some lightly dressed salad greens – lamb's lettuce, watercress, rocket, or a mixture thereof – would go well with it.

Aubergine gratin

This dish, which is found in varying forms along the Mediterranean coast, makes a good vegetarian main course.

serves 4

2 large aubergines, cut into
  1cm slices
2 tablespoons olive oil
1 onion, chopped
2 cloves garlic, crushed with a
  little salt
400g tinned chopped tomatoes
1 teaspoon dried oregano or
  2 teaspoons fresh
¼ teaspoon ground chilli or
  cayenne pepper
salt and freshly ground black pepper
125g ricotta or curd cheese
2 eggs
50g Parmesan, grated
150ml double cream

Bring a pan of water to the boil and blanch the aubergine slices, a few at a time, for 5–6 minutes until soft. Drain thoroughly. Heat the oil in a large pan and fry the onion until soft and starting to brown. Add the garlic, tomatoes, oregano, chilli and a good grinding of pepper. When the tomatoes start to bubble, reduce the heat and simmer for about 10 minutes until the mixture thickens.

Blend together the ricotta and eggs, then stir in the Parmesan and cream to make a sauce. Taste for salt and add a little if necessary.

Preheat the oven to 200°C/400°F/gas mark 6. Put half the aubergine slices into a flat ovenproof dish that will hold them side by side or just overlapping. Pour over the tomatoes. Cover with the remaining aubergines and pour over the ricotta and cream sauce. Bake for about 30 minutes until the top is golden. If the gratin is browning too quickly, reduce the heat to 180°C/350°F/gas mark 4, and if necessary cook a little longer.

Locro

Locro is a vegetable stew popular in Bolivia, Peru and Ecuador. High in the Andes there are basic versions made with potatoes, fresh white cheese and milk; in the cities locro tends to be a more complex dish. The principal ingredients are those of ancient Inca cuisine – potatoes, pumpkin or squash, corn, tomatoes, peppers. Serve locro as a main course accompanied by rice.

serves 6

50ml olive oil

2 large onions, sliced

5 cloves garlic, sliced

2kg butternut squash, peeled
and cubed

2 red chillies, seeded and sliced

400g tinned chopped tomatoes

1 teaspoon dried oregano

salt and freshly ground black pepper

200g green beans, cut into short
lengths, boiled for 5 minutes
and drained

kernels from 2 ears of corn, or
200g tinned or frozen corn

large handful of chopped coriander

Heat the oil in a large pan and fry the onions until they turn golden. Add the garlic and fry for another minute. Put in the squash, chillies, tomatoes, oregano and season with salt and pepper. Cover, lower the heat and simmer, stirring from time to time, for 20 minutes or until the squash is almost tender. If the stew starts to stick, stir in a little water. Add the beans, cover again and cook for 5 minutes, then stir in the corn. If you use fresh corn, simmer for another 5 minutes or so; if it is tinned or frozen, 2–3 minutes will be enough. Stir in the coriander and serve.

Frozen broad beans and peas are good additions to locro, and I have eaten it finished with chopped watercress, instead of coriander.

Winter vegetable stew

In all cold climates the sweet, earthy flavours of winter vegetables are enjoyed in warming stews. Celeriac, swedes, turnips, carrots, salsify, leeks, parsnips and potatoes, seasoned with spices and winter herbs and simmered in stock or a tomato broth, blend harmoniously to make a rich, satisfying meal. Any of these vegetables can replace the ones given in this recipe.

serves 6

2 tablespoons olive oil

2 onions, chopped

3 stalks celery, strings removed and sliced

2 fennel bulbs, trimmed and thickly sliced

400g tinned chopped tomatoes

150ml white wine

salt and freshly ground black pepper

400g waxy potatoes, peeled and cut into chunks

300g carrots, thickly sliced

300g turnips, peeled and cut into chunks

strip of orange peel

short stick of cinnamon

400g tinned chickpeas

Heat the oil in a large pan and fry the onions and celery gently for 10 minutes until they become limp. Add the fennel, stir carefully and fry for a further 5 minutes until softened. Put in the tomatoes and white wine, season with salt and pepper and simmer steadily for 10 minutes or so, as the alcohol evaporates and the tomatoes thicken to make a sauce. Add the potatoes, carrots and turnips, tuck in the orange peel and cinnamon and add enough water just to cover the vegetables. Cover the pan and cook until the vegetables are tender, about 30 minutes. Add the chickpeas, bring back to a simmer, taste for seasoning and cook, uncovered, for a further 5 minutes so that the liquid reduces to a sauce. Discard the orange peel and cinnamon.

Serve the stew with couscous, rice, bulgur or bread.

Catalan pasta with pork

We are familiar with Italian pasta and Asian noodles, but tend to know little about pasta in other cuisines. Spain has several good pasta dishes, many of which have been reinterpreted in Latin America. Spanish fideos, which are short lengths of spaghetti-like pasta, often form part of a substantial dish, as here, rather than being served as pasta with a sauce.

serves 4

500g pork ribs or lean pork, cut into small pieces

lard or oil, for frying

2 onions, chopped

400g tinned chopped tomatoes

¼ teaspoon pimentón (see page 118)

salt, to taste

600ml hot stock or water

for the picada

a few saffron threads

15g whole blanched almonds

2 cloves garlic, finely chopped

2 tablespoons chopped parsley

400g fideos or spaghetti, broken into short lengths

In a large pan, turn the pieces of pork in the lard or oil. When they start to brown, add the onions and cook gently for 5 minutes, then add the tomatoes. Season with pimentón and a little salt. Cook slowly until the vegetables have cooked down and thickened. Pour in the hot stock, bring to the boil and simmer for 10 minutes.

Prepare a picada by pounding together the saffron, almonds, garlic and parsley, or use a blender, moistening the mixture with a little water to make a paste.

Add the fideos to the pan, bring back to the boil and cook for 3–4 minutes. Stir in the picada and cook until the fideos are done, about 6–8 minutes.

Pasta with leek and Gorgonzola sauce

Small pasta is best for this dish; I use small shells, maloreddus, or small twists like trofie.

serves 2

2 leeks, finely sliced
2 shallots, finely chopped
1 clove garlic, finely chopped
30g butter
100ml double cream
70g Gorgonzola
salt and freshly ground black pepper
180g pasta
10 sage leaves, torn or sliced
Parmesan, to serve

To make the sauce, stew the leeks, shallots and garlic in the butter in a heavy, covered pan. They will need about 20 minutes. Stir occasionally and add a little water if they start to stick. When the vegetables are quite soft, stir in the cream and Gorgonzola, and season with pepper and a little salt, if you wish.

Put the sauce to one side while you cook the pasta in a large pan of boiling salted water for the time given on the packet. When the pasta is ready, reheat the sauce gently, if necessary, and turn the drained pasta into it. Toss to mix thoroughly and scatter over the sage leaves and a little Parmesan.

Tagliatelle with spinach and morels

Pimentón is Spanish paprika. Most comes from La Vera and carries a denomination of origin which guarantees a high-quality paprika with a smoky aroma and taste. It may be hot, sweet or bitter-sweet. In this dish, pimentón dulce, the sweet version, complements the flavour of the morels and spinach beautifully. If you use the hot version, use a little less.

serves 2

2 tablespoons olive oil
2 shallots, chopped
15g dried morels
salt and freshly ground black pepper
½ teaspoon pimentón
300g spinach, large stalks removed
2 cloves garlic, chopped
80ml double cream
200g fresh tagliatelle or pappardelle
grated Parmesan, to serve

Soak the morels in hot water for 10 minutes. Heat 1 tablespoon of oil in a pan and gently fry the shallots. Drain the morels, reserving the liquid, chop if very large, and add to the shallots. Cook for 2–3 minutes. Strain the soaking liquid, add a splash to the pan, and season with salt, pepper and pimentón. Simmer for 5 minutes. Meanwhile, roll the spinach leaves tightly and cut into ribbons. Heat the remaining oil in another pan, lightly fry the garlic and add the spinach. Season and stir-fry, turning the spinach with tongs until it wilts. Stir the cream into the morels, add the spinach mixture and mix thoroughly. Keep warm. Cook the pasta in a large pan of boiling salted water until al dente, drain well and turn into a warm bowl. Toss the pasta with the sauce and serve with grated Parmesan.

Penne with fennel, red pepper and beans

This is a satisfying, warming dish for a cold day. It tastes good without the pancetta, too, if you prefer a vegetarian dish.

serves 6

1 bunch parsley, leaves picked
3 cloves garlic, roughly chopped
1 large onion, roughly chopped
1 leek, roughly chopped
2–4 tablespoons olive oil
100g pancetta, diced (optional)
salt and freshly ground black pepper
400g tinned chopped tomatoes
350ml vegetable or chicken stock
2 heads fennel, diced
2 red peppers, seeds and ribs
   removed, diced
400g tinned haricot or cannellini
   beans, drained and rinsed
600g penne
freshly grated Parmesan

Put the parsley, garlic, onion and leek in a food processor and blend until finely chopped. Set aside.

Heat 2 tablespoons of the olive oil in a large heavy pan and sauté the pancetta until crisp. Lift out the pieces and drain on kitchen paper. Add a little more oil to the pan if necessary and sauté the chopped vegetables for 5–6 minutes, until soft. Season well and add the tomatoes and stock. Simmer for 5 minutes before putting in the fennel and red pepper. Cook the sauce for 8–10 minutes, stirring occasionally, until the fennel and pepper have lost their rawness, but still have a bite. Stir in the beans to heat through and taste for seasoning.

While the sauce is simmering, cook the penne in a large pan of boiling salted water until al dente. Drain the pasta, put it into a large bowl and toss with the sauce. Scatter the pancetta over the top and serve with the Parmesan.

Bucatini with cauliflower, raisins and pine nuts

For this traditional Sicilian dish, bucatini are used, but any long pasta is all right. The sauce is sensational and complex; the flavour of the cauliflower is transformed by the other ingredients.

Boil the cauliflower in a large pan of salted water until tender and drain, reserving the liquid. Soak the raisins and saffron separately in warm water to cover. Heat the oil in a large pan and sauté the onion until it is lightly coloured. Stir in the anchovy fillets, mashing them with a fork until they disintegrate. Drain the raisins, add the pine nuts, raisins and the saffron in its water to the pan and stir well. Put in the cauliflower florets and a ladleful or 2 of the reserved cooking water. Crush them against the base and sides of the pan with a wooden spoon until they are in very small pieces and you have a thick sauce. Season with pepper and taste to see if any salt is needed (the anchovies provide salt).

Heat the remaining cauiflower water and boil the bucatini until al dente. Drain, again reserving the liquid. Stir the pasta into the sauce, using a little of the cooking water to thin it if necessary. Serve at once with the basil leaves scattered over and grated cheese to accompany it.

serves 4

1 cauliflower, weighing about 700g,
   cut into florets

50g raisins

1/4 teaspoon crushed saffron threads

4 tablespoons olive oil

1 large onion, chopped

5 anchovy fillets, chopped

25g pine nuts

salt and freshly ground black pepper

400g bucatini

a few torn basil leaves

grated pecorino or Parmesan

Variation

To serve the cauliflower as a vegetable dish with a raisin and pine nut sauce, boil the cauliflower until almost tender. Make the sauce as described above but do not crush the cauliflower. Instead, use a little more of the cooking water to make a thinner sauce, add the florets and simmer for 5 minutes or until the cauliflower is tender. Serve garnished with basil, but omit the cheese.

Noodles with beef and broccoli

This is a version of a common Thai dish that is also made with pork or chicken, and when made there uses many more chillies. Make sure to shred the lime leaves very finely or they are impossible to eat; if you can't, it is better to leave them in large pieces and remove them before serving.

serves 4

250g egg noodles

2 tablespoons sunflower oil

3 cloves garlic, finely chopped

1 small chilli, seeded and
    thinly sliced

250g rump steak, cut into
    thin strips

200g broccoli, cut into florets

2 kaffir lime leaves, shredded

1 tablespoon fish sauce

2 tablespoons dark soy sauce

100ml stock or water

Cook the egg noodles in a big pan of boiling water until just tender, about 3–4 minutes. Drain, rinse under cold water and set aside.

Heat a wok and when it is very hot, pour in the oil, swirling it around to coat the sides. Stir-fry the garlic and chilli until the garlic is golden brown, then add the beef and stir well. Add the broccoli, lime leaves, fish sauce, soy sauce and stock. Stir and toss to coat everything in the sauce. As soon as the broccoli is tender, add the noodles. Toss everything together so that the noodles heat through, and serve.

Rice noodles with pork and crab

This dish comes from Malaysia, where the rich variety of noodle dishes draws on the food traditions of the Chinese and Malay inhabitants. The combination of pork or chicken with seafood is common, and rice noodles make this a pleasant, light dish.

serves 4

300g dried rice vermicelli

180g pork fillet, cut into thin strips

150ml stock or water

2 tablespoons soy sauce

1 tablespoon sherry

1 teaspoon sweet chilli sauce

3 tablespoons sunflower oil

2 shallots, thinly sliced

1 red pepper, seeds and ribs
   removed, thinly sliced

180g white crab meat, shredded

50g beansprouts

2 tablespoons peanuts, toasted
   and coarsely chopped (optional)

2 tablespoons chopped coriander

Soak the vermicelli for 15–20 minutes in warm water until soft, then drain. Cook the pork in simmering stock or water until just tender, and drain keeping 2–3 tablespoons of the liquid. Mix this with the soy sauce, sherry and chilli sauce and set aside. Heat a wok and add the oil, turning it to coat the sides. Stir-fry the shallots and pepper for 2–3 minutes. Add the crab meat and cook briefly, then put in the beansprouts to heat through. Add the pork and the noodles, toss and mix well. Sprinkle over the peanuts and coriander, pour over the soy sauce mixture, toss again and serve.

Roast vegetable lasagne

Roasting the vegetables makes for sharper, better differentiated flavours than if they were all sautéed together.

serves 4

1 onion, cut into wedges

½ red pepper, seeds and ribs
   removed, cut into squares

½ yellow pepper, seeds and ribs
   removed, cut into squares

Preheat the oven to 180°C/350°F/gas mark 4. Sprinkle the vegetables with a little of the rosemary and 2 tablespoons of oil and roast them for 25–30 minutes until soft. While they are in the oven, cook down the tomatoes with the remaining oil, rosemary, salt and pepper until they have thickened into a sauce.

200g butternut squash, peeled
  and cubed
1 medium aubergine, cubed
a few rosemary leaves, chopped
3 tablespoons olive oil
400g tinned chopped tomatoes
salt and freshly ground black pepper
250g fresh lasagne

for the sauce
300ml milk
20g butter
1 tablespoon plain flour
30g Parmesan or Cheddar, grated,
  plus extra to serve

Meanwhile, to make the sauce, heat the milk almost to boiling point and set aside. Melt the butter in a heavy pan and whisk in the flour. Add the milk slowly, whisking all the time until the sauce boils. Season with lots of pepper and a little salt (the cheese will be salty), put the pan on a heat diffuser and simmer gently for 8–10 minutes, stirring occasionally. Remove from the heat and stir in the cheese. Remove the vegetables from the oven and increase the heat to 200°C/400°F/gas mark 6.

Cook the lasagne in a large pan of boiling salted water until al dente, drain well and make layers in an ovenproof dish, starting with a little tomato sauce, followed by lasagne and vegetables. Continue until everything is used and finish with a layer of lasagne. Pour over the cheese sauce, grate some more cheese over the top and bake for about 45 minutes.

Red rice pilaf

Red rice cultivation in the Carmargue region of the Rhône delta has increased in recent years and it is now exported again. A medium grain rice with a slightly nutty flavour and a more chewy texture than white rice, it takes longer to cook and needs slightly more water.

serves 4–6
2 leeks, thinly sliced
1 tablespoon olive oil
300g red rice
salt and freshly ground black pepper
1 teaspoon paprika
½ teaspoon ground cinnamon
½ teaspoon ground coriander
50g raisins
juice and grated rind of
  1 unwaxed orange
50g pine nuts, toasted

Soften the leeks in the oil in a large heavy pan. Stir in the rice, salt and pepper, and spices and pour over 600ml of hot water. Bring to the boil, lower to a simmer and cook, covered, for 35–40 minutes.

While the rice is cooking, put the raisins to soak in the orange juice.

When the cooking time is up, the liquid should be almost entirely absorbed and the rice quite tender. Gently stir in the raisins and orange juice, the grated rind and the pine nuts. Put a cloth over the pan, tucking up the corners over the lid, and leave on the lowest possible heat for 10 minutes. Turn off the heat and leave to stand, covered, for another 5 minutes or more – it will stay hot for about 15 minutes.

Wild rice with mushrooms

A favourite winter dish in our household. It is best to use a variety of wild mushrooms – ceps, pieds de mouton, chanterelles, depending on availability – as well as field or portobello mushrooms. I have not found the flavours of shiitake and other oriental mushrooms to marry well with the rice. I usually serve it as a main course followed by a salad and cheese.

serves 4

90g wild rice

120g basmati rice

10g dried ceps, soaked for 20 minutes in warm water to cover

250g assorted wild mushrooms, brushed clean and sliced

250g cultivated mushrooms, brushed clean and sliced

salt and freshly ground black pepper

2 tablespoons olive oil

4 shallots, chopped

4–5 tablespoons double cream or crème fraîche

chopped parsley, to serve

Measure the volume of the wild rice and put 3 times that volume of salted water in a pan to boil. Add the wild rice, bring to the boil, lower the heat and cook gently until soft, about 50 minutes. There should be almost no liquid left in the pan.

Measure the volume of the basmati rice and soak it in warm water for 20 minutes. Drain and rinse under the cold tap until the water runs clear. For each measure of rice, pour 1 1/4 times that volume of water into a heavy-based pan. Add a little salt and bring to the boil. Add the drained rice, cover, bring back just to the boil, then put on the lowest possible heat, using a heat diffuser, and cook for 12–15 minutes. Put a clean, folded tea towel under the lid, with the corners turned up away from the heat source. Leave on the heat for 5 minutes, then turn off the heat and leave for a further 5 minutes, or longer.

Heat the oil in a large pan and cook the shallots until soft. Strain the ceps, discarding any grit and reserving the liquid. Add the fresh mushrooms to the shallots and toss and fry until the mushrooms give off their juices. Turn up the heat, season and add the ceps and 3–4 tablespoons of the reserved soaking liquid. Stir in the cream or crème fraîche, the wild rice and basmati, add a generous amount of chopped parsley and serve.

Rice with pumpkin and prunes

Dishes of rice lightly sweetened with fruit, nuts and rose water originated in Persia and the Middle East, from where they spread with the Moors to Spain and from there to Latin America. Some are baked, others cooked as pilafs, as is this one.

serves 4–6

3 tablespoons olive oil or butter

50g flaked almonds

300g basmati rice

2 small onions, chopped

1/2 teaspoon ground allspice

1/2 teaspoon ground cinnamon

1/2 teaspoon ground ginger

500g pumpkin, peeled and cubed

120g ready-to-eat stoned prunes

salt, to taste

olive oil or melted butter for the
 rice (optional)

Heat 1 tablespoon of the oil or butter in a small pan and fry the almonds, stirring, until they turn golden. Remove them and set aside to drain on kitchen paper. Measure the volume of rice; you will need 1 1/2 times that volume of water.

Heat the remaining oil or butter in a large pan, add the onions and fry until they begin to soften. Stir in the spices, then add the pumpkin and prunes. Season with a little salt and pour over the measured water. Bring to the boil, leave to simmer for 5 minutes, and stir in the rice. Bring to a lively simmer, cover the pan and put it on the lowest possible heat, using a heat diffuser, if necessary. In 12–15 minutes the rice will be almost cooked. Now, you can trickle olive oil or melted butter over the rice, or leave it plain. Put a clean, folded tea towel under the lid, turning up the corners to keep them away from the heat source. Leave the pan on a very low heat for another 5 minutes, then turn off the heat and leave undisturbed for at least a further 5 minutes, and as long as 15. The rice will stay hot. Turn it out carefully with a wooden fork and scatter over the almonds.

Gallo pinto

My younger daughter worked at a scientific research station in Costa Rica a few years ago, and often joked in her e-mails home about her daily consumption of gallo pinto, the local staple of rice and beans. When I went to visit her, it was on the menu in the dining room for breakfast, lunch, and no doubt dinner, too. I soon acquired the local enthusiasm for the dish and during our travels around the country for a couple of weeks I think we ate gallo pinto almost every day, comparing one version with another. Unlike rice and bean dishes from other parts of the Americas, the Costa Rican version is made with ready-cooked rice and beans, which is why I have given the measurements by volume rather than by weight. These proportions don't have to be precise. The name gallo pinto, by the way, means 'speckled rooster'.

serves 4–6

1 small onion, finely chopped

½ small red or green pepper, seeds and ribs removed, finely chopped

3 tablespoons sunflower oil

2 cups cooked black or red beans

3 cups cooked rice

3 tablespoons Worcestershire sauce

2 tablespoons chilli sauce, or to taste

2 tablespoons chopped coriander

4 rashers streaky bacon, fried until crisp and crumbled (optional)

soured cream (optional)

Fry the onion and pepper in the oil until the onion is soft. Stir in the beans and cook until they warm through, 2–3 minutes. Add the rice and cook for 3 minutes more. Stir in the Worcestershire sauce, chilli sauce and the coriander. Serve the gallo pinto mounded on a dish and topped with the crumbled bacon, if you wish. Sometimes it has a dollop of soured cream on the top, too.

Gallo pinto is good with fried eggs, sausages or sliced avocado.

Note
You will need roughly 300g of uncooked beans and 450g of uncooked rice to give the required quantities.

Radicchio and red onion risotto

This risotto has an attractive deep red colour. The slightly bitter taste of the radicchio is well balanced by the sweetness of the red onion and the nutty and creamy taste of the rice.

serves 4

about 1.2 litres chicken or
  vegetable stock
2 tablespoons olive oil
1 red onion, finely chopped
400g vialone rice or other
  risotto rice
1 glass red wine
salt and freshly ground black pepper
350g radicchio, shredded
30g butter
90g Parmesan, freshly grated

Heat the stock and keep it at a gentle simmer. Heat the oil in a large pan and fry the onion until it is transparent. Add the rice and stir to ensure that all the grains are coated in the oil. When the rice is hot, pour over the wine and stir until it is absorbed. Season and add a ladleful of stock, stir again and wait until it is absorbed before adding more. Continue to add the stock in this way until about half has been used. Now stir in the radicchio and as it wilts continue to add stock as before. The risotto is ready when the rice is tender and creamy but still has a slight bite at the centre; it will take about 20 minutes. Stir in the butter and Parmesan, cover the pan, remove from the heat and leave to rest for 2–3 minutes before serving.

Variation

If you like black pudding, it goes surprisingly well in this risotto. Choose one with little oatmeal, cut it into small pieces and fry gently in a dry pan to release most of the fat. Lift it out and add to the risotto just before the butter and Parmesan. For 4 servings you will need 150–200g.

Barley with Brussels sprouts and chestnuts

Barley is a cold climate crop and one of the earliest cultivated grains. It has a nutty flavour and slightly chewy texture and makes a warming, satisfying dish when combined with winter vegetables. Instead of the sprouts used here, try carrots, parsnips or pumpkin, or replace the chestnuts with 100g of lightly fried pine nuts or flaked almonds for the last 10 minutes of cooking time.

serves 4

50g butter

2 onions, chopped

250g pearl barley

650ml vegetable or chicken stock

salt and freshly ground black pepper

150g cooked chestnuts, chopped
  (see page 108)

300g small Brussels sprouts

Preheat the oven to 180°C/350°F/gas mark 4. Melt half the butter in an ovenproof casserole and fry the onions until soft. Stir in the barley and cook for 1–2 minutes to coat it with butter. Bring the stock to the boil and pour it over the barley. Season, cover the casserole and transfer it to the oven for about 45–50 minutes until the barley is almost cooked and most of the stock has been absorbed. If the liquid is absorbed before the barley is tender, add a little more stock or water. After 30 minutes, stir in the chestnuts.

Cook the sprouts in boiling salted water until almost tender, about 4–5 minutes, and drain them. Toss them in the remaining butter and stir them into the barley. Return the casserole to the oven, adding a little more stock or water should it be necessary, and cook for a further 20 minutes or until the barley turns creamy while still retaining some chewiness.

accompaniments

Broccolini with chilli and lime

If you can't get slender stalks of broccolini, buy a head of calabrese and cut it into florets.

serves 2

2 tablespoons sunflower oil

I clove garlic, sliced

I small green chilli, seeded
  and sliced

250g broccolini, trimmed

60ml chicken or vegetable stock,
  or water

salt, to taste

3 tablespoons lime juice

I tablespoon sesame oil

a few sesame seeds (optional)

Heat a wok over a high heat and when it is very hot pour in the oil. Swirl to coat the sides and add the garlic and chilli. Toss as they start to colour and put in the broccolini. Stir-fry vigorously for 2–3 minutes and add the stock or water and a little salt. Shake the wok and stir until the broccolini is just cooked, a further 2–3 minutes. Pour in the lime juice and sesame oil, toss to mix through and serve with a scattering of sesame seeds, if you wish.

Cauliflower with almonds and chilli

Although it is in season all year, cauliflower is at its best in late autumn and winter. It should be firm, ivory-coloured and have stiff, not limp, leaves. A fairly bland vegetable, it is best cooked al dente and responds well to stronger flavours, whether Indian spicing, the olives, garlic and anchovies of Sicily (see also Bucatini with Cauliflower, Raisins and Pine Nuts, page 120) or the simple treatment of almonds and chilli flakes given here. Grated pecorino could be added to the almond and chilli dressing, if you wish.

serves 4

I medium cauliflower

2–3 tablespoons olive oil

50g flaked almonds, toasted

I teaspoon chilli flakes, or to taste

Boil the cauliflower and drain while still slightly firm. Cut it into florets and discard the central stalk. Heat the oil in a large frying pan and stir-fry the florets, turning them carefully so that they colour on all sides. Scatter over the almonds and chilli flakes, turn to integrate them into the dish and transfer to a serving bowl. Serve with grilled fish or chicken.

Savoy cabbage with chestnuts

An easily prepared dish that goes well with roast meat and poultry dishes. For a richer version, you could sauté the cabbage in duck fat if you have some.

serves 6

3 tablespoons sunflower oil

1 savoy cabbage, weighing about 600g, quartered, cored and leaves shredded

75ml white wine

1/2 teaspoon ground allspice

salt and freshly ground black pepper

250g cooked chestnuts, broken into pieces (see page 108)

1 tablespoon maple syrup (optional)

Heat 2 tablespoons of oil in a heavy pan and sauté the cabbage until it softens. Add the wine and 75ml of water, season with allspice, salt and pepper, cover the pan and simmer for 15 minutes, turning occasionally. Sauté the chestnut pieces in the remaining oil until they are lightly browned. Stir them into the cabbage, continue cooking for a few minutes for the flavours to blend, and stir in the maple syrup if you intend to serve the cabbage with pork or ham. Taste and serve.

Variation

Add 75g diced bacon to the oil and let it brown lightly before adding the cabbage.

Savoy cabbage with pancetta and garlic

This recipe uses Italian flavours and oriental stir-frying to produce well-flavoured crisp cabbage. Most cabbages can be cooked in this way, but the savoy has the finest flavour.

serves 4

2 tablespoons sunflower or olive oil

100g pancetta, chopped

1 teaspoon fennel seeds

2 cloves garlic, chopped

500g savoy cabbage, stalk removed and leaves finely shredded

salt and freshly ground black pepper

Heat the oil in a large frying pan or wok and sauté the pancetta until it colours and the fat runs. Add the fennel, garlic and cabbage, toss in the oil over a high heat until the cabbage starts to wilt. Add a splash or two of water, continue cooking for 3–4 minutes, then season and serve at once.

This is good with hare and roast meat.

Swiss chard and potato

aI discovered this dish in Dalmatia, the beautiful province of Croatia that extends down the eastern Adriatic coast. The fish and seafood from the sparkling, clear waters was outstandingly good, inland there were slow-roast dishes of lamb and veal and everywhere this fine dish of swiss chard and potato. The chard did not have the broad stalks of the variety often on sale here, so if you have that type, use only the leaves and keep the stalks to add to a stew or other dish.

serves 4

500g potatoes, peeled and cut into
   large pieces

1kg chard, large stalks removed and
   leaves cut into 5cm ribbons

4 tablespoons olive oil

3 cloves garlic, chopped

salt and freshly ground black pepper

Boil the potatoes in a large pan of salted water for 10 minutes until about half cooked. Add the chard to the potatoes, bring back to the boil and cook until the chard is tender, 3–4 minutes. Drain, reserving some of the cooking water.

Heat the oil in another large pan and sauté the garlic lightly. Add the potatoes and chard, season with pepper and a little salt, if you wish. Stir to coat the vegetables with the oil. Add a ladle or 2 of the cooking liquid, crush some of the potato into it to thicken it slightly and cook until the vegetables are in a light sauce.

Serve with Roast Spiced Tuna (see page 54) or grilled lamb or fish.

Spinach with sesame

The bright colour and quick cooking make this simple dish very appealing.

serves 4

500g spinach, large stalks removed

1 tablespoon sunflower oil or
   20g butter

1 teaspoon sesame seeds,
   dry roasted

2 teaspoons sesame oil

Blanch the spinach for 1 minute, then drain and plunge it into iced water to preserve the colour. Drain thoroughly and chop coarsely. When you are ready to serve, stir-fry the spinach in the oil or butter, tossing to ensure it is evenly coated. Turn the spinach into a serving dish, scatter over the sesame seeds and drizzle with the sesame oil.

Serve with grilled or baked fish.

Red cabbage with apple and cranberries

This red cabbage dish is cooked quickly so that the cabbage retains some bite. Serve it with venison or pork, or with sausages.

serves 6

1 red cabbage, weighing about 700g, quartered, cored and leaves shredded

1 red or white onion, finely sliced

1 large tart apple, peeled and grated

3 tablespoons cranberries, fresh or dried

10 juniper berries, crushed

1 teaspoon chopped thyme leaves

salt and freshly ground black pepper

75g butter

2 tablespoons runny honey

200ml good red wine

2–3 tablespoons red wine vinegar

In a large bowl, combine the cabbage, onion, apple, cranberries, juniper, thyme and salt and pepper, and mix together well with your hands.

Heat the butter in a large pan, add the cabbage mixture, stir and turn to coat everything in the butter. Stir in the honey. Increase the heat, pour over the wine, cover the pan and cook fairly briskly for about 10 minutes. Shake or stir the pan a few times to ensure even cooking. If it is getting too dry, add a splash of water. Remove the pan from the heat, stir through the vinegar, which will give it a lively note, and serve.

Braised cavolo nero

Cavolo nero retains a firm texture after long cooking; undercooked it is decidedly chewy and tough. Red onion and garlic partner it well, and I sometimes spice it with a little ground coriander or allspice.

serves 4

3 red onions, sliced

2 tablespoons olive oil

4 cloves garlic, finely chopped

350–400g cavolo nero, tough central
   stalks removed and leaves sliced

about 300ml hot vegetable or
   chicken stock

salt and freshly ground black pepper

Sweat the onions gently for 5 minutes in the oil in a wide pan. Add the garlic to the onions, then the cavolo nero and pour over enough stock to cover the leaves by half. Season lightly. Replace the lid and braise for 20–30 minutes over a low heat, turning the cavolo nero from time to time.

Serve with venison, Braised Hare (see page 105) or Pot-roasted Beef with Mushrooms (see page 81).

Baked radicchio

This is best with the long Treviso radicchio if you can find it.

serves 4

4 heads radicchio, halved lengthways

salt and freshly ground black pepper

4–5 tablespoons olive oil

2 teaspoons balsamic vinegar
   (optional)

Preheat the oven to 200°C/400°F/gas mark 6. Cut out the central part of the radicchio stalk, leaving enough on the sides to hold the leaves together. Season lightly with salt and pepper and brush the cut side with oil. Heat a baking tray in the oven for a couple of minutes. Arrange the pieces on the tray, cut-side down, brush the tops of the radicchio with more oil and put them in the oven for about 8–10 minutes, depending on size. Turn the pieces, cut-side up, onto a warm serving dish, sprinkle with balsamic vinegar, if you wish, and serve as a separate course or to accompany meat.

Sautéed chicory and radicchio

The slightly bitter taste of the vegetables is softened by the sherry vinegar. You could use balsamic vinegar if you prefer a sweeter note.

serves 4

4 heads of chicory

2 heads of radicchio

3 tablespoons olive oil

salt and freshly ground black pepper

2 tablespoons sherry vinegar

Discard the outer leaves from the chicory and radicchio. Cut the chicory into 5mm slices. Cut the radicchio in 4, remove the central core and slice the leaves into similar-sized ribbons.

Heat the oil in a large pan or wok and sauté the chicory over a high heat for 2 minutes, tossing and stirring all the time. Add the radicchio, season and continue to toss and stir for a further 3–4 minutes until the vegetables have softened, yet still retain some crispness. Pour over the vinegar, stir for a minute longer and serve at once with grilled or roast meat or game birds, or as a separate vegetable course.

Braised chicory

Chicory is best in autumn and winter; it grows well in cool, damp conditions. Long cooking, whether steaming followed by frying gently in butter, or braising with butter, as here, produces a fine dish: the butter brings sweetness to the somewhat bitter chicory.

serves 4

100g butter

8 medium heads of chicory, trimmed

salt and freshly ground black pepper

80ml chicken or vegetable stock, or water

lemon juice

Preheat the oven to 170°C/325°F/gas mark 3. Melt half the butter in an ovenproof casserole that will hold the chicory side by side or in 2 tight layers. Turn the chicory heads, a few at a time, in the butter to coat them well. Put all of them into the pan, season, pour over the stock or water and dot with the remaining butter. Cover and braise on the stove over very low heat for 10 minutes.

Cut a piece of greaseproof paper to fit on top of the chicory, replace the lid and transfer the casserole to the oven and bake for about 1 hour. Squeeze a little lemon juice over the chicory before serving.

Mushroom ragoût

The flavour of this dish depends on the quality and variety of mushrooms and fungi used, so it is worth shopping to find four or five different ones. When I last made this, I had pieds de mouton, shiitake, oyster mushrooms, portobellos, crimini and some white button mushrooms.

serves 6

4 shallots, chopped

4 tablespoons olive oil

2 cloves garlic, chopped

2 teaspoons chopped thyme leaves

1kg assorted mushrooms, brushed
　clean and thickly sliced

salt and freshly ground black pepper

6 tablespoons crème fraîche

2–3 tablespoons chopped parsley

Sauté the shallots in the oil in a large pan for 1 minute. Stir in the garlic and thyme, and add the mushrooms. Increase the heat and stir the mushrooms frequently until they become soft. Season with salt and pepper. Stir in the crème fraîche and simmer, half covered, for 15–20 minutes until the juices thicken. Finish with some chopped parsley.

Serve as an accompaniment to veal or chicken, with Polenta (see page 161) or use as a pasta sauce.

Okra with apricots

Unlikely as this may sound, it is an excellent way of cooking okra that comes from the Caucasus, and it is very easy, too. Prunes could be used instead of apricots.

serves 4

1 tablespoon sunflower oil or
　15g butter

1 medium onion, chopped

1/4 teaspoon ground mace

1/4 teaspoon turmeric

2 tablespoons tomato purée

juice of 1/2 lemon

200ml vegetable or chicken stock

salt and freshly ground black pepper

300g small okra, stalks removed

10 dried apricots, halved

Heat the oil in a fairly heavy pan and sauté the onion until lightly browned. Stir in the spices, followed by the tomato purée, lemon juice and stock. Season with pepper and a little salt (tomato purée can be salty). Add the okra and scatter the apricots over the top. Bring to the boil, then cover and simmer for about 45 minutes.

Serve with lentils or rice, with Roast Fennel and Onions (see page 145) or with Cuban Roast Pork (see page 97).

Grilled fennel

A fast, simple way of cooking fennel, and one that converts people who normally won't touch it. If you have a ribbed griddle pan, use that instead of the grill.

serves 4
4 large heads of fennel
olive oil

Heat the grill. Remove the tops of the fennel, and keep any green feathery leaves for a garnish. Peel off the tough outer layers and cut a very thin slice from the root – you want enough root left to hold the pieces together when sliced. Slice from top to bottom, each piece about 5mm thick. Brush the slices on both sides with olive oil and grill for 2–4 minutes on each side, depending on size and how far your grill pan is from the heat source. Serve with grilled fish or chicken, or Pork Chops Baked with Sweet Potatoes (see page 98).

Roast fennel and onions

The flavours of fennel and onions complement each other and both caramelise nicely when roasted. This is a good dish to make for a large gathering, because it looks after itself. It goes well with lamb, pork and poultry, or as one of a number of dishes for a vegetarian feast.

serves 8
6 bulbs of fennel (about 1.5kg),
3 large onions, quartered
3 tablespoons olive oil
salt and freshly ground black pepper
shavings of Parmesan (optional)

Preheat the oven to 200°C/400°F/gas mark 6. Remove the outer layer and the tops of the fennel and cut the bulbs into quarters. Put the fennel and onions into a baking dish, spoon over the oil, add a little salt and mix the vegetables in the oil carefully in order not to break the pieces. It is best to do this with your hands. Roast the vegetables for 40–50 minutes, turning them 2 or 3 times. To serve, put the vegetables into a warmed dish, give a good grinding of pepper and top with shaved Parmesan, if you wish.

Gratin of Jerusalem artichokes

Sweet, nutty artichokes make a rich, luscious gratin. It can be served on its own or to accompany grilled steak or chops.

serves 4

500g Jerusalem artichokes, peeled
    and sliced

lemon juice

2 cloves garlic, crushed

250ml milk

salt and freshly ground black pepper

good pinch of nutmeg

300ml double cream

50g Gruyère, grated

Preheat the oven to 180°C/350°F/gas mark 4. Drop the artichokes into water acidulated with lemon juice to prevent discolouring. Rub one of the garlic cloves around a small gratin dish. Bring 250ml of water and the milk to the boil and add the artichoke slices. Season with salt, pepper and nutmeg and simmer gently for 6–8 minutes. They should be not quite tender.

Drain and transfer to the gratin dish. Bring the cream and both cloves of garlic to the boil in a small pan and strain it over the artichokes. Sprinkle with Gruyère and bake for about 15 minutes until bubbling and lightly browned.

Celeriac with apple and horseradish

Celeriac is one of my favourite vegetables; its flavour is more subtle than that of celery, it can be prepared in a variety of ways and it keeps well through the winter months. In this recipe, the horseradish adds a sharp, pungent note and the apple a crisp texture.

serves 4

small piece of horseradish

lemon juice

3 tablespoons soured cream

1 celeriac, weighing about
  500–600g

2 eating apples

2 tablespoons olive oil

Peel and grate the horseradish, stir a little lemon juice into it so that it doesn't brown, and stir it into the soured cream. Set aside.

Peel the celeriac, if the centre is woody discard it, and grate the flesh coarsely. Toss with lemon juice to prevent it discolouring. Peel and grate the apples and toss with a little lemon juice.

Heat the oil in a large pan and stir-fry the celeriac for 3–4 minutes. Add the apple and cook for 1 minute more, then stir in the horseradish, mixing all well together. Serve with venison and beef dishes.

Mustard leeks

A simple, easy way to prepare leeks. They go very well with baked or grilled fish and with sausages.

serves 4

2 tablespoons butter

1kg leeks, cleaned and sliced into
  1cm pieces

salt and freshly ground black pepper

1–2 tablespoons Dijon mustard

2–3 tablespoons crème fraîche or
  soured cream

Heat the butter in a wide pan and stew the leeks slowly, stirring frequently, until they are soft. Season with salt and pepper, then stir in the mustard and cream to taste.

Baked onions

Baked onions are great with pork chops or sausages. This recipe uses sliced onions, but you can bake whole small onions, or halved onions, too – they just need longer. Balsamic or sherry vinegar can be used instead of the red wine vinegar given here; whichever vinegar you use, it must be of decent quality.

aserves 4

3 tablespoons olive oil

3 tablespoons red wine vinegar

1 tablespoon chopped thyme leaves

4 large onions, sliced

2 bay leaves (optional)

2 tablespoons soft brown sugar

salt and freshly ground black pepper

Preheat the oven to 200°C/400°F/gas mark 6. Put the oil, vinegar and thyme into a large bowl and add the onion slices, coating them evenly. Transfer the onions and dressing to an ovenproof dish. Tuck in the bay leaves if you are using them, sprinkle over the sugar, salt and pepper and add 6 tablespoons of water. Cover with foil or a lid and bake for 30 minutes, then uncover and bake for a further 20–25 minutes until the onions are soft.

Gratin of winter vegetables

Gratins are very adaptable in the choice of vegetables and flavourings. Root vegetable gratins can be served as a main course, but most often accompany meats. This one goes well with Gammon Braised in Cider (see page 98) or Boeuf à la Ficelle (see page 80).

serves 4 as a main course,

6 as an accompaniment

30g butter

250g celeriac, peeled

250g parsnips, peeled

250g potatoes, peeled

salt and freshly ground black pepper

1/4 teaspoon ground allspice

300ml single cream, or half cream,
  half milk

1 clove garlic, crushed

Preheat the oven to 180°C/350°F/gas mark 4. Use half the butter to grease a gratin dish. Slice the vegetables thinly and put into the dish in layers, first celeriac, followed by parsnip and then potato. Season each layer with a little salt, pepper and allspice. Repeat the layers until all the vegetables are used. Heat the cream with the garlic, strain it over the vegetables and dot with the remaining butter. Cover the dish with foil and bake for 30 minutes, then remove the foil and bake for a further 20–25 minutes until the top is browned and the centre of the gratin can easily be pierced with a skewer.

Variation
Make your own choice of 3 or 4 vegetables: carrots, swedes, turnips or sweet potatoes can all be used instead of those I've chosen.

Provençal lentils

Lentils are available in several varieties; the ones with the best flavour and texture come from Puy in France and from Castelluccio in Italy. Decidedly comfort food, they respond well to a variety of flavourings: herbs, spices, cream or yogurt, as well as the traditional garlic and tomato of Provence.

serves 4

250g Puy lentils

3 tablespoons olive oil

I onion, chopped

2 cloves garlic, chopped

I bay leaf

½ teaspoon crushed black
   peppercorns

I tablespoon tomato purée

salt, to taste

I tablespoon chopped mint

I tablespoon chopped parsley

Pick over the lentils and wash them. Heat the olive oil in a large pan and sauté the onion until softened and translucent but not browned. Add the garlic, stir it in the oil for a moment, then put in the lentils, bay leaf, peppercorns and tomato purée. Pour in 750ml of water, stir to mix in the tomato purée and cook, partly covered, until the lentils are tender; this should take 20–25 minutes. Check the pan from time to time and add a little more water, if needed, to keep the lentils covered.

Add a little salt in the last 5 minutes of cooking. Drain the lentils well, discard the bay leaf and stir in the herbs and a little olive oil, if you wish.

Serve with Roast Rack of Lamb with Dukka (see page 92). With other dishes such as Okra with Apricots (see page 143), Grilled Fennel or Roast Fennel and Onions (both on page 145) and a beetroot dish (see opposite); it makes a good vegetarian meal.

Beetroot with yogurt dressing

Yogurt and beetroot combine well, and the freshly ground coriander seed gives the dish a pleasantly woody, tangy aroma and an orange-like flavour *(see photo overleaf, left)*.

serves 4

350g beetroot, peeled and grated

4 tablespoons thick yogurt

I teaspoon ground coriander seeds

Drop the beetroot into boiling salted water for 5–6 minutes; it should retain some bite. Drain the beetroot and turn it into a dish, stir in the yogurt, add the ground coriander and serve.

This goes well with game birds, hare or the Tourtière (see page 102).

Beetroot with balsamic vinegar and dill

If you have good aged balsamic vinegar, use a few drops of it in this dish; if you have one of the less expensive ones use 2–3 tablespoons *(see photo overleaf, right)*.

serves 4

2 tablespoons olive oil

350g raw beetroot, preferably
   small, peeled and finely grated

balsamic vinegar (see above)

2 tablespoons chopped dill

Heat the oil in a wide pan and sauté the beetroot for 4–5 minutes. Stir in the balsamic vinegar, garnish with dill and serve with duck or pork dishes. Cold, it makes a good salad.

Glazed sweet potatoes

Deep orange-coloured sweet potatoes have a soft moist flesh that responds well to sweet flavours (honey, maple syrup, fruit juices), and to alcohol (rum, whisky, cognac, port). With this in mind, and perhaps the addition of warming spices – allspice, cinnamon, cloves, ginger, quatre-épices – this dish can be endlessly varied.

serves 4

750g sweet potatoes, peeled and
   cut into chunks
juice and grated rind of
   1 unwaxed orange
2 tablespoons honey
2 teaspoons balsamic vinegar
4 tablespoons port
salt and freshly ground black pepper
1 teaspoon ground ginger
50g butter

Preheat the oven to 180°C/350°F/gas mark 4. Put the sweet potato chunks in a single layer in a baking dish. Whisk together the orange juice, honey, balsamic vinegar, port and seasoning. Scatter the orange rind over the sweet potatoes, pour over the liquid and dot with small pieces of butter. Bake the potatoes for 1–1¼ hours until soft and golden.

Baste them regularly, especially during the first half of the cooking period. If the glaze is becoming very sticky, lower the heat for the last 15 minutes or so.

This is good with Rabbit with Prunes and Almonds (see page 107), Gammon Braised in Cider (see page 98) and with roast duck or pork.

Baked sweet potatoes

Try these as a change from ordinary baked potatoes. For each person, choose a potato weighing about 200g. Scrub them, pierce a few times with a fork, put them on a baking tray and bake for 40–50 minutes in the oven preheated to 180°C/350°F/gas mark 4. Serve with roast pork or ham.

Squash purée

Winter squashes – acorn, butternut, crown prince, *kabocha* – make fine-flavoured purées in different shades of gold. Butternut has the lightest texture, *kabocha* the most dense. All squashes respond well to spicing: allspice, cardamom, cinnamon, coriander seed and ginger are the ones I use most, sometimes with a dash of whisky or rum, sometimes with honey and lemon juice, or just with butter and cream, as here. Hard-skinned squash can be roasted whole if you prick the skin a few times. The timing depends on the size and variety of the squash, but as a guide, a 1kg squash will need about 1¼ hours at 200°C/400°F/gas mark 6. The squash is ready when it collapses easily when you push it.

serves 4

1 squash, weighing about 1.5kg,
   halved lengthways and seeded
sunflower or olive oil
¼–½ teaspoon ground coriander
salt and freshly ground black pepper
50–60g butter
100ml double cream or
   crème fraîche

Preheat the oven to 190°C/375°F/gas mark 5. Brush the squash flesh with oil and bake the 2 pieces in the oven for 30–45 minutes, depending on the variety and size. Remove the flesh and purée it with the coriander, salt, pepper and butter. Add the cream, a little at a time, to make a smooth, but not runny, purée.

Serve with Guinea Fowl with Blackberry Sauce (see page 74), Duck with Vanilla (see page 73) or Rabbit with Prunes and Almonds (see page 107).

Caramelised parsnips

Parsnips readily take up sweet flavours, so it is easy to vary this dish. Try maple syrup instead of honey or substitute sesame oil or a nut oil for the butter. For a sweet-sour note, add a splash of sherry vinegar. Young parsnips can be brushed with the glaze and finished under the grill.

serves 4

500g parsnips, peeled and halved
   lengthways
60g butter
salt and freshly ground black pepper
good pinch of ground ginger
2 tablespoons honey

Preheat the oven to 180°C/350°F/gas mark 4. Blanch the parsnips in boiling water for 3–5 minutes, depending on their age. Drain and cut into thick slices. Lighly butter a wide ovenproof dish and put in the parsnips in 1 layer. Season them with salt, pepper and ginger. Heat the remaining butter in a small pan, add the honey and let it bubble up. Drizzle the liquid over the parsnips, transfer the dish to the oven and bake for 10–12 minutes until the parsnips are tender and glazed.

These parsnips go well with Cuban Roast Pork (see page 97) and Guinea Fowl with Blackberry Sauce (see page 74).

Parsnip cakes

Parsnips' natural sweetness combines well with spices and herbs. These parsnip cakes can be flavoured with ground mace, coriander or ginger, or among herbs try thyme, dill, mint or the chopped green leaves from bulbs of fennel. Finely chopped spring onions or watercress are another possibility.

serves 6

500g parsnips, peeled and cut into
   small pieces
about 40g butter
salt and freshly ground black pepper
1/2 teaspoon mace, or to taste
2 tablespoons plain flour
1 egg, beaten
breadcrumbs, for coating
oil, for frying

Boil the parsnips in lightly salted water until soft. Drain and mash with the butter, some pepper, mace and up to 1 tablespoon of flour. The texture should be firm but not too stiff. Shape the mixture into round flat cakes, dip each one into the remaining flour, then the beaten egg and coat with breadcrumbs. Heat a little oil in a large frying pan and fry the cakes over a low heat until golden brown on both sides.

Serve hot with Guinea Fowl with Blackberry Sauce (see page 74), with Pot-roasted Beef with Mushrooms (see page 81) or as part of a vegetarian meal.

Jansson's temptation

I first ate this immensely popular Swedish dish at the house of Swedish friends and found it quite wonderful. The saltiness of the anchovies gives flavour to the potatoes, and the cream adds a delicate note. Do not omit or reduce the number of anchovies, they are essential to the dish and not over-whelming. If you use salted anchovies, soak them for about 30 minutes to remove excess salt, and fillet them. Tinned anchovy fillets may need rinsing if very salty, otherwise they can be used straightaway.

serves 4–6

40g butter

6 medium waxy potatoes, peeled and thinly sliced

1 large onion, finely chopped

12 anchovy fillets, cut into pieces

250ml double cream

Preheat the oven to 200°C/400°F/gas mark 6 and butter a gratin dish with half the butter. Arrange half of the potatoes in the dish and cover with the onion and anchovies. Top with the remaining potatoes. Smooth the top and pour over the cream. Dot with the rest of the butter and bake in the oven for 50–60 minutes. If the top is browning too quickly, cover with foil. Leave the dish for a few minutes before serving, because it will be very hot.

This is one of those dishes that seems best on its own, or with salad or other vegetables, rather than with meat. I suggest Baked Onions (see page 148) and Braised Cavolo Nero (see page 141) as possible accompaniments.

Gratin savoyard

This gratin differs from the better-known gratin dauphinois in being made with stock and cheese, not cream. It produces a rich, sustaining dish that can be eaten on its own with a salad or to accompany roast meat. Local Beaufort cheese is standard, but another firm mountain cheese such as Gruyère can be used.

serves 4

about 90g butter

500g waxy potatoes, peeled and
   thinly sliced

salt and freshly ground black pepper

pinch of nutmeg

90g Beaufort or Gruyère, grated

150ml chicken or vegetable stock

Preheat the oven to 180°C/350°F/gas mark 4. Butter a gratin dish generously and add a layer of potatoes. Season with salt, pepper and nutmeg, scatter over some cheese and dot with a little butter. Continue with the layers finishing with a layer of cheese. Pour over the stock, dot with butter, cover with foil and bake for 30 minutes. Remove the foil and return the dish to the oven for a further 20–30 minutes. Stick a skewer into the gratin to check that the potatoes are tender all the way through; the stock should all have been absorbed. Leave to stand for a few minutes, because it will be very hot.

Serve with Seared Venison Medallions with Sage Butter (see page 103). It is also good with game birds, Slow-roast Leg of Lamb (see page 91) and Pot-roasted Beef with Mushrooms (see page 81).

Variation
Soak 30g of dried ceps in warm water for 20 minutes, drain and chop them and put a layer through the centre of the gratin.

Mash

One of the most comforting foods imaginable, mash is quick to make and goes just as well with grilled fish or sausages as with a fortifying stew or a grand roast. A plain, buttery potato mash is fine in itself, but many flavours can be added to suit the dish it is to accompany. Other winter vegetables – celeriac, fennel, parsnip, turnip – used half and half with potato make good mashes. Irish colcannon has cooked shredded cabbage beaten into a mash made with milk.

Instead of butter or milk, make the mash with cream or crème fraîche, yogurt, olive oil or a nut oil. Nutmeg, mace, ginger and turmeric are good seasonings; saffron gives a musky flavour to olive oil mash, and a dash of Pernod livens up a potato and fennel mash. Other favourite additions include roasted garlic, a teaspoon or two of Dijon mustard or pesto, and to accompany fish make a mash with grated lemon rind, lots of chopped parsley and a little lemon thyme. I've included a recipe for horseradish mash (below); vary your mash to suit the meal you are preparing.

Horseradish mash

serves 4
3 large potatoes (500–600g), peeled
   and quartered
50g horseradish
150ml crème fraîche or
   soured cream
salt and freshly ground black pepper

Boil the potatoes until tender. While they are cooking, peel and grate the horseradish. Drain the potatoes, mash them together with the horseradish and add the cream. Season and serve with beef, pork or smoked fish.

Note
Peeled horseradish freezes well and you can grate off as much as you need while it is frozen and return the rest of the root to the freezer.

Polenta

Pre-cooked polenta needs only about 5 minutes soaking in the prescribed amount of water. It lacks the texture and taste of slow-cooked polenta, but it will do if you are in a hurry. Real polenta demands more time and attention.

serves 4–6

1 teaspoon salt

300g polenta

1 tablespoon olive oil or
   15g butter

Bring 1.5 litres of water to the boil with the salt. As soon as it boils, pour in the polenta meal slowly, whisking hard. Don't stop whisking otherwise the grains may stick together, and make sure the water remains at a steady boil until all the polenta is in the pan. It will bubble violently. Reduce the heat to very low and simmer for about 30 minutes, stirring frequently with a wooden spoon, always in the same direction, to prevent a skin forming on top. When it is cooked, the polenta will have absorbed all the water and will pull away from the sides of the pan. Stir in the olive oil or butter.

Soft polenta

If you intend to serve the polenta soft, leave it to rest for 5 minutes, then put it into a bowl and serve with more olive oil or butter and grated Parmesan, or as an accompaniment to a stew.

Firm polenta

When the polenta is cooked, pour it into a lightly greased shallow baking tin to make a layer about 1.5cm thick. Smooth the surface, cover with a sheet of greaseproof paper and leave to cool. When it is firm it can be cut into squares or slices. Brush these with olive oil and toast or fry, or use as layers in a composite dish; see the suggestions below.

Sausages go well with both sorts of polenta; the Mushroom Ragoût (see page 143) is very good with firm polenta.

Polenta with olives   Slice about 20 stoned black olives and stir these into the polenta just before it is cooked; or top grilled slices of plain polenta with green or black olive paste and serve as a snack.

Polenta with herbs   Stir a teaspoon of chopped rosemary or thyme leaves into the polenta just before it is cooked; or fry slices of plain polenta in oil flavoured with sage leaves.

Polenta with cheese   Stir 60g of grated Parmesan into the polenta just before it is cooked; or top grilled slices of polenta with a paste of mashed Gorgonzola, butter and a splash of cognac; or layer firm polenta in an ovenproof dish with grated Gruyère and dabs of butter and bake at 180°C/350°F/gas mark 4 for 15–20 minutes.

desserts

Lemon ice cream

This ice cream has a lively yet delicate flavour, and provides a refreshing end to a substantial winter meal. I've made it using all double cream, also with a mixture of thick yogurt and cream and with a mixture of cream and crème fraîche. I find this last the most successful; the slight sharpness of the crème fraîche complements the acidity of the lemon juice. On occasion I have added a slug of lemon-flavoured vodka; this takes longer to freeze because of the alcohol, and should be put in the freezer for an hour after blending.

serves 6

3 large or 4 small unwaxed lemons

150g caster sugar

250ml double cream

250ml crème fraîche

Grate the peel from the lemons, combine it with the sugar in a food processor and blend until the sugar becomes cream-coloured. Squeeze enough of the lemons to produce 6 tablespoons of juice and add this to the sugar. Whizz again so that the sugar starts to dissolve in the juice. Mix together the double cream and crème fraîche, stir in the juice and sugar and chill for 30 minutes. Taste and add a little more juice if necessary, then freeze in an ice cream machine following the manufacturer's instructions.

This is quite a soft ice cream and is best eaten the day it is made.

Cinnamon ice cream

Spiced ice creams go well with many winter tarts and other desserts, or can be served on their own with an almond biscuit. The basic custard can be used with a variety of flavours – see the suggestions below.

serves 6

300ml single cream or full milk

1 tablespoon ground cinnamon

4 egg yolks

150g granulated sugar

300ml double cream

Bring the single cream or milk slowly to the boil with the cinnamon. Remove the pan from the heat, cover, and leave to infuse for 20 minutes. Whisk the egg yolks and sugar until thick and pale. Gently reheat the cream, pour a little into the yolks, then pour this mixture into the pan and return it to a very low heat. Stir for several minutes until the cream is thick enough for your finger to draw a line on the spoon. Do not let the mixture boil or it will curdle. Should that happen, lift the pan from the heat at once, add a spoonful of cold milk or cream and beat hard; this usually remedies it.

Whip the double cream lightly and fold it into the custard. Freeze in an ice cream machine following the manufacturer's instructions. If you do not eat the ice cream straight away, put it in a plastic container in the freezer and transfer it to the refrigerator for 30 minutes before serving.

Vanilla ice cream

Infuse a split vanilla pod in the single cream for 30 minutes, strain and continue with the recipe.

Clove and crystallised orange ice cream

Add 1/4 teaspoon ground cloves to the single cream; there is no need to leave to infuse. Stir 100g of diced crystallised orange peel into the custard just before adding the double cream. If you wish, you could also add 2 tablespoons of an orange liqueur at this stage.

Cardamom ice cream

Lightly crush 6 green cardamom pods and infuse them in the single cream for 30 minutes, strain and continue with the recipe.

Whisky and ginger ice cream

This is a rich, festive ice cream. Because of the alcohol content, the ice cream needs longer to freeze than the time allowed in an ice cream maker, so it should be transferred to the freezer for a while before serving.

serves 6

75ml granulated sugar

75ml bourbon whisky

100g preserved ginger,
   finely chopped

4 egg yolks

100g caster sugar

450ml full milk

150ml double cream

Bring 75ml of water and the granulated sugar to the boil in a small pan, stirring to dissolve the sugar. Simmer for 5 minutes, then cool. Add the whisky and ginger and set aside.

Beat the egg yolks and caster sugar until pale and thick. In another pan, heat the milk slowly just to boiling point. Pour a little into the egg and sugar mixture, beating all the time. Add the rest of the milk slowly, and keep stirring. Return the mixture to the pan over a low heat and stir until it is thick enough for your finger to draw a line on the spoon, but do not let it boil. Strain into a bowl and stir as the custard cools, then stir in the ginger mixture.

Whip the cream lightly and fold it into the custard. Freeze in an ice cream maker, according to the manufacturer's instructions, then put the mixture into a plastic box and leave in the freezer for at least 1 hour before serving. It will be soft enough to serve straight from the freezer.

Spiced syllabub

Make this pretty, dusky pink syllabub the day before you want to eat it. In fact, all syllabubs will keep for 2–3 days in a cool place or the refrigerator.

serves 8

250ml decent red wine

1 stick cinnamon

8 cloves

90g caster sugar

rind of 1 unwaxed lemon

rind of 1 unwaxed orange or

  2 unwaxed tangerines

300ml double cream

sprigs of rosemary or crystallised

  rose petals, to decorate

Put all the ingredients except the cream and rosemary into a pan and bring slowly to the boil. Pour into a bowl, cover and leave to infuse for 12–24 hours.

Strain into a large bowl and add the cream slowly, stirring all the time. Whisk until the mixture thickens and holds a soft peak on the whisk. It will take several minutes. Spoon into glasses, and refrigerate or put in a cool place until needed. Put a small sprig of rosemary or a few crystallised rose petals on the top of each one before serving.

Cranachan

I first came across this traditional Scottish dessert some years ago in Theodora Fitzgibbon's *A Taste of Scotland*. At the time I was looking for dishes using oatmeal, and exploring books on Scottish food seemed a good place to start. And so it proved – oatmeal pastry, oatmeal soup, haggis, oatcakes, and cranachan. I was intrigued by the name, and found it to be a fresh-tasting dessert of nutty oatmeal and whipped cream, flavoured with honey, a dash of whisky or rum and soft fruit. I was hooked.

serves 4

2 heaped tablespoons medium

  oatmeal

250ml double cream

1–2 tablespoons whisky or rum

2–3 teaspoons honey

120g blueberries or blackberries

Toast the oatmeal in a heavy frying pan until it is lightly browned. Let it cool. Whip the cream until it starts to hold its shape, stir in the whisky or rum and honey to taste. Fold in the oatmeal. Pile the cranachan in glasses and chill in the refrigerator for at least 30 minutes. Top with blueberries or blackberries just before serving.

Queen Mab's pudding

This splendid pudding is based on a recipe in Eliza Acton's *Modern Cookery*, published in 1845. Queen Mab was queen of the fairies to most 16th-century poets; in *Romeo and Juliet* she is the fairies' midwife who gives birth to dreams; Ben Jonson, in *Entertainment at Althorpe*, calls her 'mistris-Fairie':

'This is Mab, the mistris-Fairie,
That doth nightly rob the dayrie;
And can hurt, or helpe the cherning,
(As shee please) without discerning.'

Whatever she got up to in the dairy, Mab's pudding suggests it was good rather than evil.

serves 8–10

oil, for brushing

600ml full milk

rind of 1 small unwaxed lemon, without pith

½ vanilla pod, cut in 1cm pieces

15g powdered gelatine

120g caster sugar

300ml double cream

6 egg yolks, well beaten

50g crystallised orange or citron peel, finely chopped

90g preserved ginger, finely chopped

90g pistachio nuts, chopped

ginger syrup from the preserved ginger, to serve

Brush a 1 litre mould with a flavourless oil, and turn it upside down to allow excess to drain off.

Heat the milk slowly with the lemon rind and vanilla pod. Simmer gently until the milk is well flavoured, about 15–20 minutes. Sprinkle over the gelatine and stir. When the gelatine has dissolved, strain into a clean pan.

Stir in the sugar and cream and bring just to the boil. Stir the mixture – 'briskly and by degrees', says Miss Acton – into the beaten egg yolks. Pour it back into the pan or stand the bowl containing the mixture over a pan of simmering water and stir until it thickens to a custard thick enough to coat the back of the spoon. Do not let it boil or it will curdle. Remove from the heat and stir until it is cool.

Add the crystallised peel, ginger and pistachios and turn the mixture into the mould. Chill until set. Turn the pudding out to serve and pour round it some of the syrup from the ginger jar.

Prune and armagnac ice cream

I first tasted this sensational ice cream at Berthillon, the excellent ice cream shop on the Ile St Louis in Paris. The best French prunes come from Agen in southwest France in the heart of armagnac country, so the marriage of prunes and armagnac is a combination of two of the region's finest products.

makes about 1 litre
75g granulated sugar
75ml armagnac
250g ready-to-eat stoned prunes
4 egg yolks
125g caster sugar
500ml full milk or single cream

Bring 75ml of water and the granulated sugar to the boil, stirring to dissolve the sugar. Simmer for 5 minutes, then add the armagnac. Bring to the boil, add the prunes, remove the pan from the heat, cover it and leave to infuse for 1 hour. Purée the mixture in a food processor and set aside.

Whisk together the egg yolks and caster sugar until thick and pale. Heat gently the milk or cream, pour it onto the egg yolks, whisking steadily. Return the mixture to the pan and simmer gently, stirring to thicken, until the custard coats the back of the spoon. Do not let it boil. Strain into a bowl and keep stirring until the mixture cools. Set the food processor running again and add the custard to the prune purée through the funnel, a little at a time.

Freeze in an ice cream machine, following the manufacturer's instructions. Transfer the ice cream to a plastic container and put it into the freezer for at least 1 hour before serving. Because of the alcohol, it will not freeze hard and can be served straight from the freezer.

Prunes in port and orange syrup

Like the ice cream opposite, this recipe comes from Agen in southwest France. Make the dish at least a day before you wish to eat it.

serves 6–8

300g sugar

1 stick cinnamon

1 vanilla pod, split

200ml ruby port

juice and grated rind of 1 large
   unwaxed orange

500g ready-to-eat stoned prunes

Heat together the sugar, cinnamon, vanilla pod and 700ml of water. Bring to the boil once the sugar has dissolved, then simmer for 6–8 minutes. Remove the pan from the heat, stir in the port, orange juice and rind and pour over the prunes. Cover and leave in a cool place for 24 hours.

The next day strain off the liquid into a pan, bring to the boil and keep over a high heat until it has reduced by half. Pour over the prunes again and leave to cool. Serve straightaway or if you prefer, chill first. Serve with Cinnamon or Vanilla Ice Cream (see page 165).

Dried fruit compote

This fragrant compote of dried fruit, flavoured with rose or orange flower water, is one of our family favourites. It can be made just with apricots and raisins, but we like to include other fruit – peaches, pears, prunes or figs. The dish must be macerated for 48 hours, and will keep longer. We often eat it for breakfast if any is left over from dessert.

serves 6–8

300g dried apricots

120g sultanas

120g raisins

150g dried peaches

150g dried figs

caster sugar (optional)

2 tablespoons rose or orange
   flower water

100g pistachio nuts, or blanched,
   flaked almonds

Put all the dried fruit into a large bowl and cover with water. Taste and add sugar if you like very sweet things. Add the rose or orange flower water, cover and put the bowl in the refrigerator for at least 48 hours. Just before serving, stir in the nuts.

Variation

To flavour the compote, use the grated rind of an unwaxed orange and a small stick of cinnamon instead of flower water.

Poached quinces with mascarpone

It is a pity that quinces have been forgotten in England; quince trees used to be common, as were quince desserts and preserves, although we did not adopt the Moroccan, Turkish and Iranian ways of using them with meat. They are available from Middle Eastern shops, some greengrocers and supermarkets. They are best picked or bought slightly unripe and left to mature in a warm kitchen until yellow and scented, when they are ready to be cooked.

serves 4

300g granulated sugar

juice of 1 lemon

peel of 2 unwaxed oranges,
    blanched twice

2 vanilla pods, split

4 medium quinces

150g mascarpone

2–3 tablespoons honey (optional)

Preheat the oven to 150°C/300°F/gas mark 2. Put 1 litre of water, the sugar, lemon juice, orange peel and vanilla pods into a pan. Bring to the boil and simmer for 15 minutes. Transfer the syrup to an ovenproof casserole. One at a time, peel the quinces, cut them in half and remove and reserve the cores. As soon as each one is ready put it into the syrup to avoid discolouration. Tie the cores up in a piece of muslin and add this to the casserole. Put a double piece of greaseproof paper over the quinces to keep them under the surface of the syrup. Cover the dish and bake in the oven for about 1 ½ hours until the quinces are soft.

Lift the fruit from the syrup and put them in a serving dish. Discard the bag of cores and the orange peel and boil the syrup to reduce it to a coating consistency. Spoon this over the quinces and let them come to room temperature. Leave the vanilla pods in the dish as a garnish.

To serve, sweeten the mascarpone with honey to taste, if you wish, and fill the cavities of the quinces with the mixture.

Baked quinces

For this recipe, choose quinces that are of a similar size, and preferably not too large. If they are huge, serve one for two people.

serves 6

6 semi-dried figs, chopped

2 tablespoons sultanas

1 tablespoon honey

1/2 teaspoon ground cinnamon

6 quinces

lemon juice

50g butter

3 tablespoons double cream

Preheat the oven to 170°C/325°F/gas mark 3. Combine the figs with the sultanas, honey and cinnamon. Peel and core the quinces, painting them with lemon juice as you do so to prevent discolouration.

Melt most of the butter and coat an ovenproof dish into which the quinces will fit snugly. Brush the outsides of the quinces with the rest of the melted butter and stand them in the dish. Stuff them with the fig mixture, put a dab of the remaining butter on top of each one and bake for 45 minutes to 1 hour, depending on size. Baste once or twice with the juices in the dish. 10 minutes before the quinces are ready spoon a little cream into the filling. Serve hot or warm.

Roast figs

Do not use very ripe figs for this dish or they may collapse when cooked. A muscat wine gives the figs a good flavour.

serves 4

butter

8 firm figs, stalks removed

2 tablespoons caster sugar

1/4 teaspoon ground cinnamon

pinch of ground cardamom

juice and 2 strips of peel from
   1 unwaxed orange

80ml sweet wine

Preheat the oven to 200°C/400°F/gas mark 6. Butter a baking dish just big enough to hold the figs. Stand them in the dish and sprinkle over the sugar and spices. Discard the pith from the strips of orange peel, and tuck them between the figs. Pour over the orange juice and the wine and put the dish in the oven for 20–30 minutes, depending on the ripeness of the figs.

Transfer the figs to a serving dish. If there is too much liquid to spoon over the figs, put it in a small pan and reduce it a little first. Serve hot or cold.

Orange and almond cake

This cake, which is more like a dessert than a cake, is a traditional dish of the Sephardi Jews. The recipe comes from Claudia Roden's magnificent *A Book of Middle Eastern Food*. I make it following Claudia's recipe, but also with blood oranges or with four aromatic mandarins, following the suggestion of a good friend, Dr Joy Lake, at whose home in Sydney I have often eaten it.

serves 8–10

2 large unwaxed oranges

butter and plain flour, for the tin

6 eggs

150g caster sugar

2 tablespoons orange flower water

250g ground almonds

1 teaspoon baking powder

Wash the oranges and boil them whole for 1½–2 hours, or until they are very soft. Lift them out and leave to cool, then cut them open, remove the pips and purée in a food processor.

Preheat the oven to 190°C/375°F/gas mark 5 and butter and flour a 24cm springform cake tin. Whisk the eggs with the sugar until light and trebled in volume. Stir in the orange flower water, almonds and baking powder. Mix the orange purée into the egg and almond mixture and pour into the tin. Bake for 1 hour; if it starts to burn cover the top with foil. Leave to cool in the tin before turning out.

Sticky date pudding

A really sticky, rich pudding that originated at the Sharrow Bay Hotel in the Lake District.

serves 6–8

75g butter, plus extra for greasing

200g dates, stoned and chopped

1 teaspoon bicarbonate of soda

175g caster sugar

2 eggs

175g self-raising flour

1 teaspoon vanilla extract

for the sauce

300ml double cream

75g demarara sugar

50g butter

Preheat the oven to 180°C/350°F/gas mark 4 and butter a 22cm square baking tin. Boil the dates in 250ml of water until they soften, about 4–5 minutes. Remove the pan from the heat, add the bicarbonate of soda and set aside. Cream the butter and sugar until fluffy, beat in the eggs, one at a time, and fold in the flour. Mix in the vanilla extract, the dates and their liquid. Pour the mixture into the tin and bake until firm to the touch, about 30 minutes.

While the pudding is baking, put all the sauce ingredients into a pan and bring to the boil, stirring slowly. Pour a little of the sauce over the pudding and put it back in the oven for 2–3 minutes so that it forms a glaze. Cut the pudding into squares and serve with the remaining sauce.

Louisiana bread pudding

This Louisiana favourite, with its bourbon whisky or cognac sauce, has become a staple in our household ever since I sampled four or five subtly different versions on a visit to New Orleans. Some versions have no pecans, others put them into the sauce; some sauces are made in the classic brandy butter fashion with alcohol, butter and icing sugar; some, like mine, include cream. I urge you not to use Scotch for the sauce. Bourbon has a different flavour; if you don't have any, use cognac instead.

serves 6

500ml full milk

50g butter, plus extra for greasing

50g granulated sugar

1/2 day-old French loaf, cubed

80g raisins

80g pecan nuts, chopped

2 eggs

1/2 teaspoon grated nutmeg

1 teaspoon vanilla extract

for the sauce

150ml single cream

1 teaspoon cornflour

30g caster sugar

1/2 teaspoon vanilla extract

3 tablespoons bourbon whisky

Heat the milk, then remove from the heat, add the butter and sugar and stir until the butter has melted and the sugar dissolved. Add the bread and raisins and leave to stand for 15 minutes. Preheat the oven to 180°C/350°F/gas mark 4. Add the chopped pecans to the bread mixture. Whisk the eggs, add the nutmeg and vanilla and pour into the bread mixture. Mix thoroughly. Grease a medium baking dish, tip in the mixture and bake for 35–40 minutes.

To make the sauce, mix a little of the cream with the cornflour, put this and the rest of the cream into a small pan with the sugar and vanilla extract. Heat through gently until the sauce thickens slightly. Stir in the whisky, simmer for a minute or so more and serve the pudding with the sauce.

Persimmon pudding

In winter, vivid orange persimmons hang on leafless trees around the Mediterranean – a sparkling sight against a darkening sky. These fruit, that look somewhat like tomatoes, have thin skins, a pulpy flesh and sometimes contain seeds. Until completely ripe, the tannins in the flesh make persimmons too astringent to eat, so make sure you choose fruit that are soft with no green or yellow patches. Sharon fruit, a variety developed in Israel, is less astringent and can be eaten while firm, so it is good for salads, but it lacks the real sweetness of a fully ripe persimmon. This recipe comes from Ann Arnold, a fine still-life painter and talented cook, who lives in Berkeley, California.

serves 6–8

600g ripe persimmons

90g butter, plus extra for greasing

125g caster sugar

2 eggs

3 tablespoons cognac

1 teaspoon vanilla extract

1 teaspoon cinnamon

100g raisins or currants

2 teaspoons bicarbonate of soda

150g plain flour, sifted

Cut around the calyx of the persimmons and remove it, then cut the fruit in half. Scoop out the flesh with a spoon, discarding any seeds, and blend to a purée. You should have about 450g.

Preheat the oven to 170°C/325°F/gas mark 3. Butter a 22cm soufflé dish or pudding basin and line the bottom with greaseproof paper. Beat the butter and sugar together until fluffy, then whisk in the eggs. Fold in the persimmon purée followed by the brandy, vanilla, cinnamon and raisins. Dissolve the bicarbonate of soda in 2 tablespoons of hot water and stir this in. Finally fold in the flour. Pour the mixture into the dish, and cover tightly with a double layer of greaseproof paper, tied around the top if necessary.

Bake in a bain-marie of boiling water for 2–2¼ hours. Top up the bain-marie with hot water, if necessary, and if the pudding seems to be browning too quickly lower the heat. Let it stand for 15 minutes before turning out.

Serve the pudding with whipped cream laced with cognac, or with Vanilla or Cinnamon Ice Cream (see page 165).

Sweet potato pie

This may sound odd, but think American pumpkin pie. Potato pies, sweetened with honey and later with sugar, were popular with our ancestors, and this version, made with sweet potatoes, draws on the flavours of orange flower water and cinnamon used in early English cooking.

serves 6

for the shortcrust pastry

200g plain flour, plus extra
   for dusting

1/4 teaspoon salt

2 teaspoons caster sugar

100g butter, cut into small pieces

1 egg yolk, lightly beaten (optional)

3–4 tablespoons iced water
   (more if needed)

for the filling

500g sweet potatoes, peeled,
   boiled and mashed

80g brown sugar

25g butter

3 tablespoons double cream

2 tablespoons brandy

1 teaspoon ground cinnamon

pinch of ground cloves

1 tablespoon orange flower water

3 egg yolks

2 egg whites

Make the pastry following the same method as Blueberry Tart (see page 184) using a 24cm tart tin. Set aside. Preheat the oven to 200°C/400°F/gas mark 6.

While the potatoes are still warm, stir in the sugar, butter and cream, followed by the brandy, cinnamon, cloves and orange flower water. Whisk the egg yolks in a separate bowl and stir in. Beat the whites to soft peaks and fold in. Turn the filling into the pastry case and bake for 20 minutes, then lower the heat to 150°C/300°F/gas mark 2 and bake for a further 15 minutes.

The tart is best served at room temperature, alone or with whipped cream laced with rum, or with Cinnamon Ice Cream (see page 165).

Blueberry tart

Alsace has a long tradition of baking sweet and savoury tarts. Onion tart and flammekueche are the best known savoury tarts; when it comes to desserts, all the fruit of the region's orchards find their way into tarts. It is best to use a metal tin, preferably one with a removable base, for making tarts. Heavy porcelain dishes do not transfer heat well enough, and tarts are difficult to turn out.

serves 8–10

3–4 tablespoons fine white
    breadcrumbs or biscuit crumbs
600g blueberries
100g caster sugar, plus extra to finish
2 eggs
100ml single cream or crème fraîche
caster sugar, to finish

for the shortcrust pastry
250g plain flour, plus extra
    for dusting
¼ teaspoon salt
2 teaspoons caster sugar
125g butter, cut into small pieces
1 egg yolk, lightly beaten (optional)
5–6 tablespoons iced water
    (more if needed)

First make the pastry. Sift the flour and salt together, then mix in the sugar. Rub the butter into the flour with your fingertips until the mixture has the texture of fine breadcrumbs. Make a well in the centre, add the egg yolk or a little iced water and mix quickly to a dough with a knife. Add more water gradually, if necessary. Bring the dough together with your fingers, and knead gently for 1–2 minutes on a lightly floured board. Shape the pastry into a ball, wrap in clingfilm and refrigerate for at least 30 minutes to allow it to relax.

Preheat the oven to 200°C/400°F/gas mark 6. Roll out the pastry and line a 30cm tart tin. Prick the pastry several times to prevent it bubbling up while baking. Scatter the crumbs over the base to absorb any excess juice, and cover them with the blueberries. Sprinkle with 30g of sugar and bake the tart for 15–20 minutes.

Make the custard topping while the tart is in the oven. Beat the eggs with the rest of the measured sugar, making sure the sugar has dissolved. Whisk in the cream gradually. Pour the mixture over the tart and bake for a further 12–15 minutes, or until the custard is set. Sprinkle caster sugar over the tart and leave to cool. Serve cold, but not chilled.

Variation

To make the pastry using a food processor, pulse the flour, salt and sugar to sift. Add the butter in small pieces and pulse for 5–10 seconds. Add the egg yolk if you are using one and pulse again. Sprinkle over iced water, using half the amount given above, pulse once or twice and gradually add a little more water, if needed. Pastry made in a food processor requires less liquid than pastry made by hand. As soon as the pastry starts to form a ball, take it out, knead briefly until smooth, then wrap and refrigerate for 30 minutes.

Serious chocolate cake

Chocolate has no claim to being a winter ingredient, but a rich chocolate cake is the ultimate comfort food, so it seemed legitimate to include a recipe. I made a version of the classic French almond and chocolate cake with chopped brandied prunes, which was well received by the family – until I made this one, which is utter indulgence, the quintessential chocolate cake. The vote was unanimous. The recipe comes from Jeremy Lee, chef at the Blueprint Café at London's Design Museum. He published it in the *Guardian* as Gâteau Ste-Victoire.

serves 8–10

240g fine bitter chocolate

6 eggs

110g caster sugar

250ml double cream

1 teaspoon vanilla extract

100ml strong rich coffee

3 tablespoons dark rum

60g good cocoa powder

Preheat the oven to 170°C/325°F/gas mark 3. Line a round 24cm baking tin with greaseproof paper, or use a greased 24cm plastic mould from which the cake will detach itself easily. Put it into a roasting tin in which it fits snugly. Break the chocolate into a spotlessly clean bowl, and place it over a pan of simmering water. Without stirring or permitting moisture to touch the chocolate, leave it to melt.

Whisk the eggs and sugar until they are pale and greatly increased in volume. In another bowl, whisk the cream with the vanilla extract until soft peaks form. Stir the melted chocolate into the eggs and add the coffee and rum. Sift the cocoa powder into this mixture and fold in, along with the cream and vanilla. Pour the mixture into the prepared tin. Pour hot water into the baking tray to come halfway up the sides of the cake tin. Bake on the middle shelf of the oven for 25–30 minutes – it will still appear soft in the centre – and leave to cool in the tin or on a rack.

Note

As there is no flour in this cake, it is fragile, so it requires care to turn out and when slicing. It is best to use a hot knife for each cut, although the cake becomes more firm after 24 hours, and then slices more easily.

Chocolate walnut torte

This is a rich confection that always seems to meet with approval. Chop the fruit by hand, rather than in a food processor, because that tends to produce pulp rather than separate pieces. The texture of the torte is quite soft and sticky, so it is best made a day before it is eaten, to allow it to become firmer.

serves 6–8

120 walnuts, chopped

60g dates, stones removed, chopped

60g dried apricots, chopped

60g crystallised citron or orange peel, chopped

60g glacé cherries or pineapple, chopped

180g caster sugar

3 tablespoons plain flour

1 teaspoon baking powder

¼ teaspoon ground cinnamon

2 eggs

60g good-quality dark chocolate, grated

butter and plain flour, for the tin

Preheat the oven to 150°C/300°F/gas mark 2. Mix together the walnuts, dates, apricots, citron or orange peel and cherries or pineapple. Sift together the sugar, flour, baking powder and cinnamon. Beat the eggs until pale and fluffy and mix in the sugar and flour mixture. Add the nut and fruit mixture along with the chocolate. Mix well. Pour into a well-buttered and floured 22cm cake tin, smooth the top and bake for 45–50 minutes until the torte is golden brown. Cool on a rack and serve with whipped cream.

Imperial equivalent of metric measurements used in this book

Weight (solids)

15g	½oz
25g	1oz
40g	1½oz
50g	1¾oz
75g	2¾oz
100g	3½oz
125g	4½oz
150g	5½oz
175g	6oz
200g	7oz
225g	8oz
250g	9oz
275g	9¾oz
300g	10½oz
325g	11½oz
350g	12oz
400g	14oz
425g	15oz
450g	1lb
500g	1lb 2oz
600g	1lb 4oz
700g	1lb 9oz
750g	1lb 10oz
1kg	2lb 4oz
1.2kg	2lb 12oz
1.5kg	3lb 5oz
2kg	4lb 8oz
2.25kg	5lb
2.5kg	5lb 8oz
3kg	6lb 8oz

Volume (liquids)

15ml	½fl oz
30ml	1fl oz
50ml	2fl oz
100ml	3½fl oz
125ml	4fl oz
150ml	5fl oz (¼ pint)
200ml	7fl oz
250ml (¼ litre)	9fl oz
300ml	10fl oz (½ pint)
350ml	12fl oz
400ml	14fl oz
425ml	15fl oz (¾ pint)
450ml	16fl oz
500ml (½ litre)	18fl oz
600ml	20fl oz (1 pint)
700ml	1¼ pints
750ml (¾ litre)	1½ pints
1 litre	1¾ pints
1.2 litres	2 pints
1.5 litres	2¾ pints
2 litres	3½ pints
2.5 litres	4½ pints
3 litres	5¼ pints

Length

5mm	¼ inch
1cm	½ inch
5cm	2 inches
7cm	3 inches
10cm	4 inches
15cm	6 inches
18cm	7 inches
20cm	8 inches
24cm	10 inches
28cm	11 inches
30 cm	12 inches

Index

Ingredients are shown in roman type, recipes in *italics*. Not included are garnishes, cooking fats and oils; a few ubiquitous ingredients (onions, garlic, etc) are listed only when essential or in unusual quantity. Recipes which are suitable for vegetarians have the letter v after the page reference; recipes which *can* be suitable for vegetarians have (v) after the page reference.

Scallops with winter vegetables page 50

Roast goose with prunes and apples page 70

Queen Mab's pudding page 170

Acknowledgements

Thanks go first to my husband, Paul Breman, who has eaten his way through the book, offering suggestions and advice. He also organised the typescript into presentable form and compiled the index. I much appreciate Kyle Cathie's continuing faith in the idea for this book; since a conversation many years ago she has encouraged me, patiently, to write it.

   Thanks to Caroline Taggart for her constructive editing and support; to Jason Lowe for his instinctive understanding of the book and his fine photographs; to Vanessa Courtier for the wonderful design and art direction; to Sunil Vijayakar and his assistant Tanya Sadourian, for cooking and presenting all the dishes for photography; to Vanessa Kendell for meticulous copy-editing. Thanks also to Renata and Raffaele Giacobazzi and to Sabrina Rippon who generously lent dishes, pans and cloths for photography, to supplement those belonging to myself, Vanessa and Jason.

   I could not have worked with a more enthusiastic or agreeable team.